GIVE PUPPETS ANOTHER HAND

Violet Whittaker

BAKER BOOK HOUSE Grand Rapids, Michigan 49506

ACKNOWLEDGMENT

Thanks again to my dear friends and coworkers who made writing plays, constructing puppets, finding props, and practicing programs fun. A special thanks goes to my chief typist, Alice Bronson. Donna Harrison also typed several of the plays. Many of the puppets pictured in this book were designed and made by Estalene Brown, without whose help these plays never would have gotten off the printed page. Not least are those faithful puppeteers, the college students, who so graciously performed for us all.

Photographs by Mike Bartlett

To my children:

Jim
Shannon
David
and
Nancy

who even enjoy
seeing the same show
more than once.

CONTENTS

A BIT OF PUPPET PHILOSOPHY

Over the last few years we have established some basic principles for using puppets in Christian work. Although each person must develop his own philosophy about the kind of puppet work he plans to do, perhaps our ideas will serve as guidelines to help you establish yours.

We never have a puppet of Christ. Somehow it doesn't seem reverent to bring our God down to a puppet level. This obviously limits us when we would like to teach about Christ in the New Testament. But we can have a voice from the sidelines. An example of a play like this could be from Mark 3 where Christ says to the man with the withered hand, "Stretch forth thy hand." The whole play could revolve around the trials of the crippled man until he found Christ, and then portray the man's joyous reward upon obeying the command.

We try not to have a puppet get "converted" or "saved from sin" (whatever term we use to express the new life we find in Christ) *on stage.* After all, a puppet is only a puppet (however real he becomes to the audience) and Christ died for real live people. Emphasize that! Sometimes, in order to teach the truth or show that a life is changed when it comes into contact with Christ, a conversion experience is implied. But that must be followed up when you, as a teacher, carry through with the explanation to the audience.

We keep our puppets alive! They are never left lying around for children to see or play with. As soon as a show is over, the puppets go back into their boxes. Once I saw a puppeteer (not one of ours) take a little puppet off his hand and thunk its poor head against the edge of the table to prove to the children that it wasn't real. This was meant to precede the discussion time of how Christ died for real people, not puppets—but imagine how all of the children in the audience felt with their dreams dashed to pieces. They were not listening to anyone at that point, but rather were trying to recover their mental composure. Don't destroy a puppet's life-likeness.

We give a puppet a personality that is consistent with his "character." Exaggeration helps. For example, if he's happy, he's *really* happy. If he's sad, he's *really* sad. If he asks questions, he asks *a lot* of questions. Enjoy thinking through the personality that the author intended for each character in a play. That's why it's important to know all of the parts, not just the puppet's part that you plan to perform.

We speak articulately and slowly. The audience needs to hear each word by itself because puppets don't have moving mouths to follow. (We all do more lip reading than we realize.) Therefore, each word must be deliberate and distinct.

We make sure the script reads smoothly. Any part of a script that doesn't seem natural to you should be revised until it does feel natural. Each person must have some leeway as he reads or memorizes his part. One word of caution, however: Don't deviate too far from the original script or you will lose the author's intended tone.

The reason for a Bible puppet show is to illustrate a Bible truth, not to entertain — although I trust some of the stories will have entertaining features. Children should be forewarned as to what kind of show to expect. If they expect laughs and clowning, they may be disappointed. But if they are told, "This story is from the Bible and it really happened like this long ago," the story can be intriguing. Esther is an excellent example of a play which shows how God's truth triumphs over the plots of wicked men.

There are many ways to use puppets. One idea is to have a personable little character who "shows up" some time each week just to talk with the children. He's really a wonderful teacher, and can say so much more than the real instructor. A puppet can also be used to put on a "one-man show" with a stage, lights, and all the trimmings. Most important, puppets can be used like the characters in this book. On stage, before an eager audience, they come to life in the hands of trained puppeteers.

Adjust by gathering around neck of puppet.

GARMENT
cut two

place on fold of fabric

PUPPET HAND
cut four

Use felt to match face color.

Stitch two pieces together to form each mitten-hand, then turn inside out.

BASIC PATTERN FOR HAND PUPPETS

To attach felt hand to garment, turn garment wrong side out. With thumb up, insert felt hand (right side out) into sleeve until raw edges are together (see illustration). Sew around the edge of sleeve opening with an overcast stitch, easing material to fit. Turn garment right side out.

A suggested fabric for basic outfits is double knit. It will stretch to fit most hands without binding, and is especially good for puppet's "wrist area" (the little hands should fit snugly on the puppeteer's finger and thumb). This pattern may be adjusted to fit operator's hand.

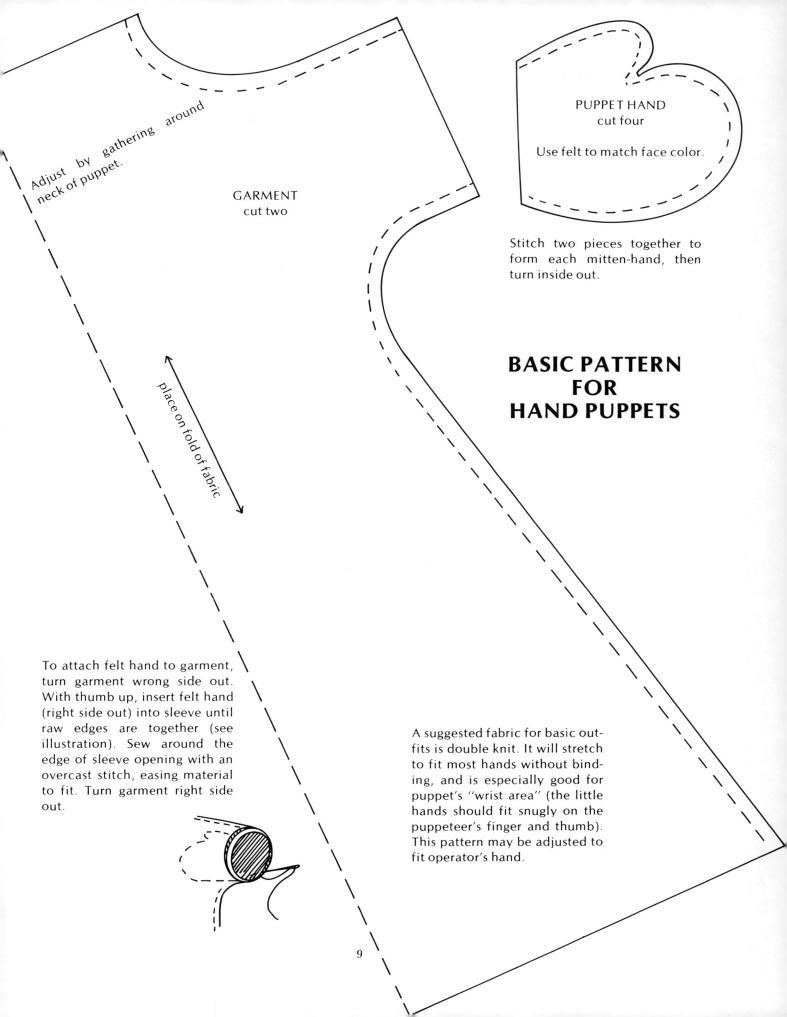

9

MAKING PAPIER-MACHÉ PUPPET HEADS

You will need the following materials:

styrofoam ball (3″ or larger)
instant papier-maché
lightweight cardboard
acrylic paint
white glue
yarn or theatrical hair

Construction procedures:

Cut a wedge out of the ball. This will be the area for the forehead.

Flatten the sides slightly by pressing the ball on the countertop (unless you want the head to be perfectly round). Use a gentle rolling motion to round off the sharp edges.

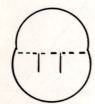

Cut two slits on the front, one at each side of the nose area. With your thumbs, press the cheek areas round.

Shape the nose, any style. More styrofoam can be added. Use toothpicks or broom straws to attach.

 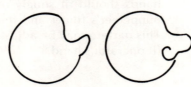 

10

With knife, carve hole in base of puppet for neck area. Be sure to have the hole centered and straight up. Remember that the puppet head will be held by your finger and must fit over both finger joints.

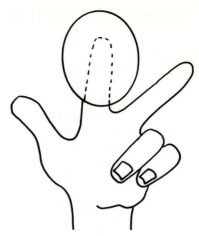

Insert a strip of lightweight cardboard (approximately 3″ x 5″) into the neck opening. Tear the cardboard edges (do not cut), so you won't hurt your finger when you put the puppet on.

Adjust the cardboard to fit comfortably around your index finger, allowing one-inch to protrude for the neck. Secure with tape.

Mix the instant papier-maché with water until it is of dough-like consistency. Cover the puppet head and neck with papier-maché. Sometimes this goes on easier if it has been mixed a day or two earlier. Be sure to add a rim around the base of the neck to hold the clothes on. Features such as ears, chins, and noses may be added now, or later after the puppet head has dried. Place puppet head upright on a stick to dry. (Stick may be placed in a bottle or vase). When head is completely dry, paint with acrylics. Add hair and eyebrows.

Theatrical or crepe hair may be purchased from a theatrical supply company, such as:
Stagecraft Industries
P.O. Box 4442
Portland, Oregon 97208
phone 503-226-7351

Instant papier-maché and styrofoam balls are available where arts and craft supplies are sold. They can also be ordered from a crafts company, such as:
American Handicrafts Co.
4300 N.E. Sandy Blvd.
Portland, Oregon 97213
phone 503-288-5701

MAKING FELT PUPPET HEADS

You will need the following materials:

felt (use different shades and colors for different races. Allow extra material for matching hands.)
felt-tip pens or acrylic paints
theatrical hair, yarn, or fake fur
cotton balls for stuffing
white fabric glue (available in fabric shops or hobby corners)

Construction procedures:

Machine sew two head pieces together with small stitches. Turn inside out. Stuff with cotton. Add features with felt tip pens, or paint with acrylics. Glue on hair. Sew robe onto neck. Attach hands to robe. Add headdress.

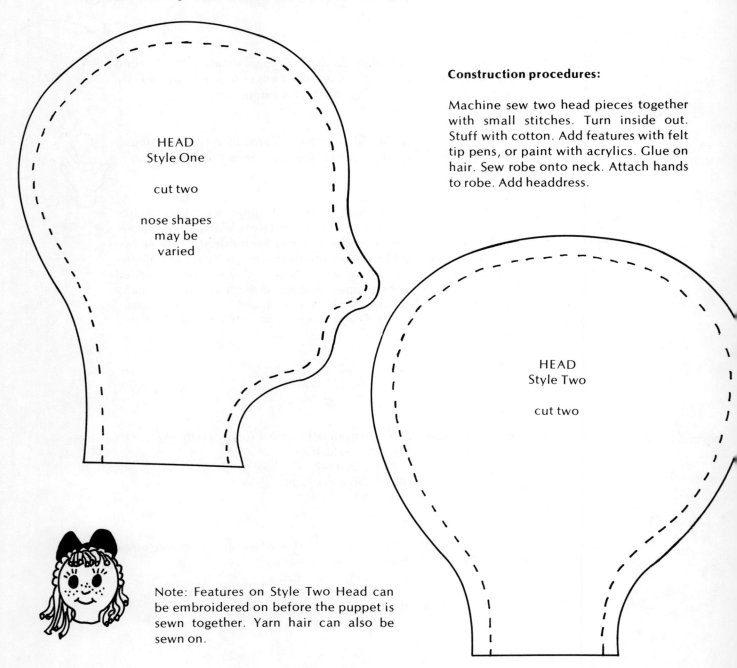

HEAD
Style One

cut two

nose shapes
may be
varied

HEAD
Style Two

cut two

Note: Features on Style Two Head can be embroidered on before the puppet is sewn together. Yarn hair can also be sewn on.

HAVE FUN WITH HEAD SHAPES

The basic head pattern can be altered
to suit many personalities.

Experiment with some paper patterns. The most fun of all is making noses.
Begin with the basic pattern, then make some changes.

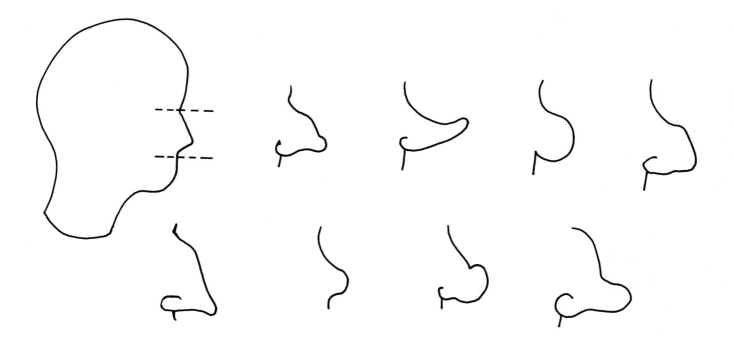

Are you getting your own ideas now? As you experiment with different facial
features you will create some delightful puppets.

Pattern for Doll-face Felt Puppets

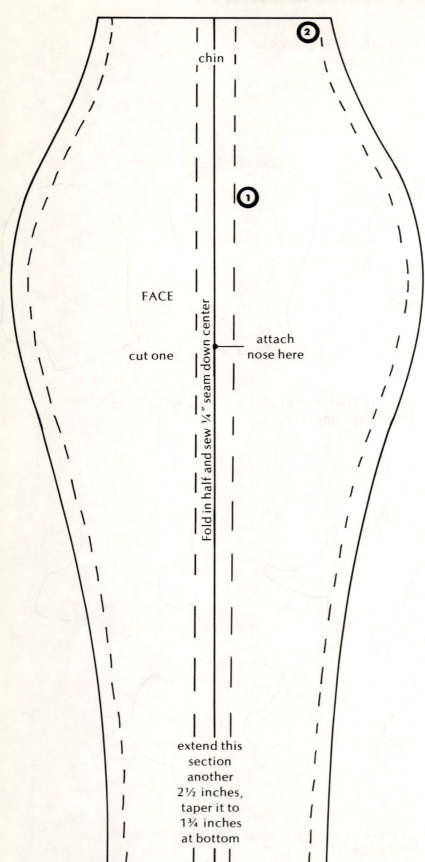

chin

②

①

FACE

cut one

Fold in half and sew ¼" seam down center

attach
nose here

extend this
section
another
2½ inches,
taper it to
1¾ inches
at bottom

Sewing directions:

The pattern pieces will just fit on a 9 x 12 felt piece. Cut out. Sew center seam on face piece (1). Attach side piece by starting at chin edge (2). Sew around. Attach second side piece also by starting at chin edge also (2). Turn right side out. Center seam bulk should be on inside. Gather-stitch around nose, pad with bit of cotton, draw up into ball. Whip-stitch together and attach to center seam. Stuff head. Add mouth and eyes. Stitch on yarn hair. Sew onto gown.

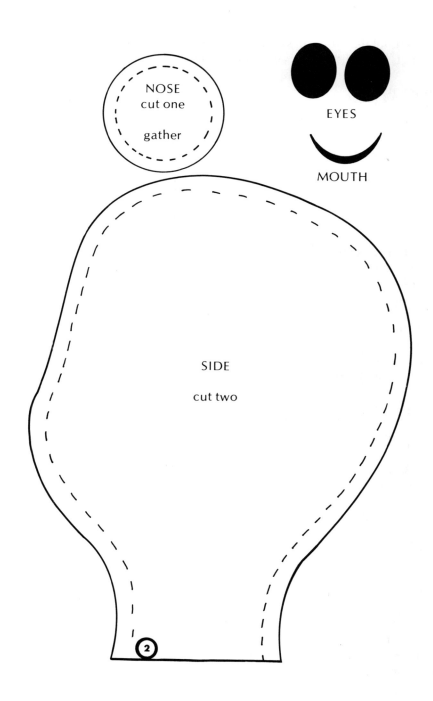

NOSE
cut one

gather

EYES

MOUTH

SIDE

cut two

2

15

MAKING BACKDROPS FOR A PUPPET STAGE

You will need the following materials:

pellon: medium weight or light medium weight
(Use a material that you can see through slightly because you will need to know where the puppets are on stage as you operate them from your position behind the backdrop.)
acrylic paints
sponges
small paint brush for details

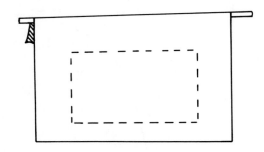

Construction procedures:
Cut pellon to desired size for backdrop. Remember to make it larger than the stage opening. Allow extra room at top and sides, or audience will see you through the gap when the puppets are performing.

Sketch design on pellon with lead pencil or chalk. Place several layers of newspaper under the backdrop to be painted. The excess moisture will soak down into the papers.

Mix acrylic paint with water in a shallow container until desired consistency is reached. Use a diluted paint mixture for skies and other large areas. Use concentrated paint mixtures for close-up areas such as tree trunks, branches, flowers and other details.

Use a big sponge to apply the large areas of color such as sky. Load the sponge and gently sweep it all the way across the pellon strip. You may want to practice on an extra piece of pellon to see what effects different sponge and brush strokes make. Work from the background (distant objects) to the foreground. Allow one colored area to dry before adding another, since colors may run.

Paint trees with a heavily-loaded sponge and dab color on thick. Make tree trunks and branches with a long, swiping motion. Paint fine details and outlines with the brush.

Make backdrops simple. Too many bright colors and details will detract from the puppets. Just remember that a backdrop is a background and only suggests the idea for the settings.

Always roll backdrops for storage. Never fold them. They may be rolled onto a long paper tube and stored in a plastic "sleeve."

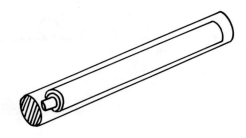

Enlarging a picture:

Choose the sketch you want.

Decide how much larger it needs to be — three times larger, four times, five times, etc.

Block off the large backdrop and smaller picture into the same number of sections.

Fill in one square at a time, as it corresponds to the squares in the smaller drawing.

Let's make it five times larger

Divide lengths and widths into five equal parts, each part the size of the original drawing.

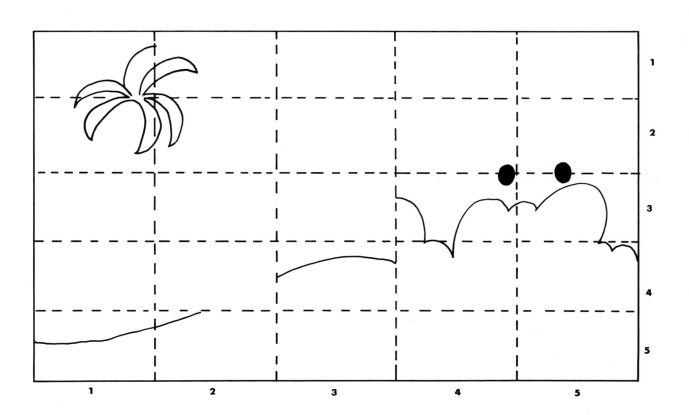

THE PARABLE OF THE SEED AND THE SOIL

A puppet play from Matthew 13:1–23; Mark 4:1–20; and Luke 8:4–15.
8 short acts

Characters:
- Twelve seeds
- A big hand (gloved)
- Feet walking over seeds
- Bird that looks like devil
- Roadside soil
- Rocky soil
- Thorny soil
- Good soil

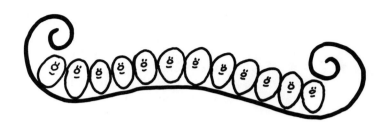

Scene One: Twelve seeds, on a scroll of white, wait to be planted.

Seeds: Isn't it great to be so important?
We can make the whole world beautiful!
And happy.
We grow.
And we bring life.
We multiply.
And increase.
Sometimes a hundred times a hundred.
We want to be accepted.
And understood.
And shared.
And spread around everywhere in the whole world (*Hand reaches down and takes three seeds out.*)
Oh, this is so exciting!
I wonder what kind of soil we will get?
I can hardly wait to begin to grow and multiply.
(Curtain)

Scene Two:

Roadside soil: Life is nothing but the same old rut day after day. Nothing but pound, pound, pound. (*Feet go across in heavy work shoes.*) I get so tired of people walking all over me! It's terrible to be treated this way. It would be nice to have a change of pace. (*Feet go across in dainty shoes.*) It doesn't make any difference. I'm so worn out I can't stand it. (*Seeds are dropped on him.*) What's this? More traffic! Oh, yikes! I'm so tired of being bothered. If I just ignore this, whatever it is, maybe it'll go away.

19

Seeds:
Ouch! It hurt to land here.
It hurt me, too.
Me, three.
I wonder if this is good soil for seed?
It hasn't said anything to us yet.
No response at all.
Let's tap a little and get its attention.
(*Seeds bounce.*)
I don't think we can grow very well here. This ground seems so hard and packed.
Let's try to get our roots in.
Maybe we can just scratch the surface.
(*Seeds make scratching movements. Add sound effects.*)

Soil:
I don't want any seeds on me! It's apt to make me change! Take it away!
(*A bird comes on stage and takes the seeds away one by one.*)

Soil:
I don't mind being walked on. I know I get trampled all the time and nobody cares about me, but at least I'm used to it.
(*Curtain*)

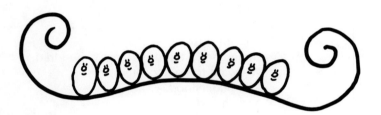

Scene Three: Nine seeds wait to be planted.

(*Hand reaches down and takes three seeds out.*)
Oh, this is so exciting!
I wonder where we will land?
I can hardly wait to begin to grow and multiply.
(*Curtain*)

Scene Four:

Rocky soil:
Oh, boy, life is nothing but the same old rocky existence, day after day after day. Nothing but rocks here, rocks there, rocks everywhere. Will there ever be anything to brighten my life?

(*Seeds are dropped on soil.*)
What's this? More rocks? Oh . . . no . . . it looks like seeds. Good! Something that can grow in me and change me! Hi, seeds, welcome to my rocky top.

Seeds: Hi. Thank you! We are eager to begin growing. Are you sure it's all right if we grow on you?

Rocky Soil: Of course, glad to have you. I need a change of lifestyle. Too much rock is not good, you know.

Seeds: We'll do our best to bring about some changes. We'll just let our roots snuggle down deep into the warm rich soil that . . .(*Trails off.*) there doesn't seem to be much soil here. Maybe we can survive on a little bit. We'll try.

Rocky Soil: Do your best! But don't move any of my rocks. I'm good enough just the way I am. I couldn't take too many changes. In fact, my friends wouldn't like it if I changed. I've got to please them, you know. Who wants to be persecuted for being different.

Seeds: We can't make it here, fellas. We're goners for sure. We could have helped him if only he had given us a chance to grow.
(*They fall over and die.*)

Rocky: Well, it's back to being the original rock-strewn soil for me.
(*Curtain*)

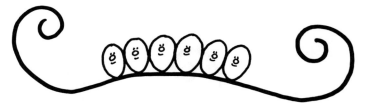

Scene Five: Six seeds wait to be planted.

(*Hand reaches down and takes three seeds out.*)
Oh, this is so exciting!
I wonder what kind of soil we will get?
I can hardly wait to begin to grow and multiply!
(*Curtain*)

Scene Six:

Thorny soil: It's good to have something growing on me. I wouldn't want to be bare, empty soil. No! I want to have everything I can get. The more the better.

(Seeds are dropped on the thorny soil and land on tiny thorns.)

Seeds:
Ouch!
This hurts.
What is it?
I'm not sure what kind of soil we have landed on, but it sure has prickers. This may be difficult, but perhaps we can grow here.

Thorny Soil:
Hello, you're some kind of seeds, aren't you? Welcome to my soil. Stick around and grow, if you like. I'm glad to have you. The more the better, I always say.

Seed:
Thank you. But you already have something growing on you.

Thorny Soil:
Oh, that's just some little thorn bushes. I don't think there will be any problem. There'll be room for all.

Seed:
Thank you. We'll try. Just let us snuggle down in the soil and we will begin to grow.

Thorny Soil:
(Worried.) I really wonder if I can offer everything that I said I could. Maybe there won't be room for both seeds and thorns. And the thorns were here first. *(Thorns pop up a little higher.)* I need to keep my prior commitments. Oh, dear! Life is such a worry. There's always some kind of problem. *(Thorns pop up higher.)* If I don't manage—I'll never be rich, and I do so want to be rich, not just kind of rich—but really rich. *(Thorns pop up higher yet.)* There is probably more profit in thorns than there is in those seeds. *(Thorns pop up still higher.)* Those seeds probably won't make it. *(Seeds choke and topple over.)* Well, I tried to keep both.

(Curtain)

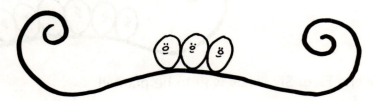

Scene Seven: Three seeds wait to be planted.

(Hand reaches down and takes out last three seeds.)
Oh, this is so exciting!
I wonder what kind of soil we will get?
I can hardly wait to begin to grow and multiply!
(Curtain)

Scene Eight:

Good Soil:
Such a nice day! Maybe something special will happen to me today. I like adventure.

(Seeds are dropped on the good soil.)

Seed: Oh, good! This is a happy landing!
It's so soft!
I feel welcome.
Good, then maybe we can snuggle down here.
And grow.
And multiply.

Good Soil: Well, hello there! Who are you? Seeds, huh? Well, well! Welcome to my soil! Put your roots down here. I'm so glad to have you! Can you stay a long time? *(Seeds nod.)* You can! Good! I have a zillion questions to ask you. Who put you here?

Seed: The sower.

Good Soil: But why did he choose me?

Seed: Because he loves you.

Good Soil: He does? Wow! *(Pause.)* Am I the only soil he loves and puts seed on?

Seed: Oh, no. He loves all kinds of soil and spreads his seed everywhere, but many of them don't really want to have anything to do with the seed He brings.

Good Soil: Not me! I'm glad you're here! After all, what good is soil anyway, if it doesn't have anything growing in it. Besides, I want good stuff growing in me. Who knows what may happen!

Seed: Something good will happen.

Good Soil: What can I do to help you grow?

Seed: You're already doing it. Just by welcoming us, and inviting us to put our roots down here. We can grow and multiply and you will experience joy.

Good Soil: I like that idea! Thank you for coming—and don't ever leave.
(Curtain)

Narrator: In the Bible, we read that Jesus told this story to the multitude. People did not understand what He meant so He explained it to those who asked. The seed is God's Word. God is the one who plants it. The seed is sown on all kinds of soil. The soil represents all kinds of people. Sometimes Satan snatches the seed away. Some people don't want to hear God's Word; they don't care what happens to it and other interests crowd it out. Others let sin choke it out. But some want to hear God's Word and accept it with joy and it blesses them and multiplies. There are four kinds of soil: Roadside, Rocky, Thorny, and Good. What kind of soil does God find you to be?

PATTERN FOR SEED PUPPETS

You will need the following materials:
    velour (or similar fabric)
    thread
    stuffing
    movable eyes (1 or 1½ cm. in diameter)

Construction procedure:
Cut out a front, back, base and nose for each seed. Run a gathering stitch around the nose piece, pull up and stuff. Sew nose together. Tack it to the center front. Add the center tuck to face. Sew two sides of base to bottom of back, right sides together. Sew back to front with right sides together, leaving bottom end open. Reverse and stuff. Add weight to bottom, if desired, and stitch closed by hand. Glue on eyes. A felt mouth may be added. The seed puppets should vary somewhat in size and features.

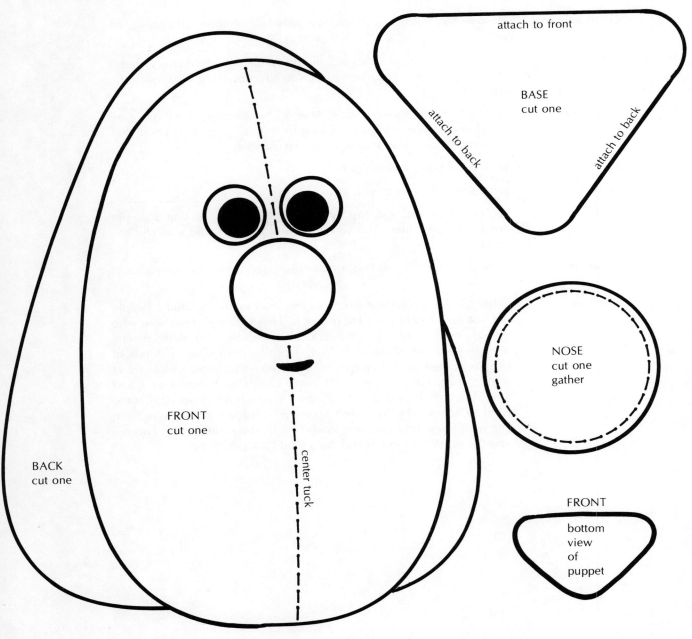

DIRECTIONS FOR SOIL PUPPETS

Use two 18" × 18" x 3" pieces of foam (the kind used to make furniture seats). Cut the square of foam in two with an electric knife, zig-zagging to make it appear eroded. Use the rippled side for the front. Cut a slit (with the electric knife) from the back to the front and through some of the center front to make a mouth. Pull out bits of foam from the back to make a pocket for the operator's hand. Failure to do this will make the soil bulge when occupied.

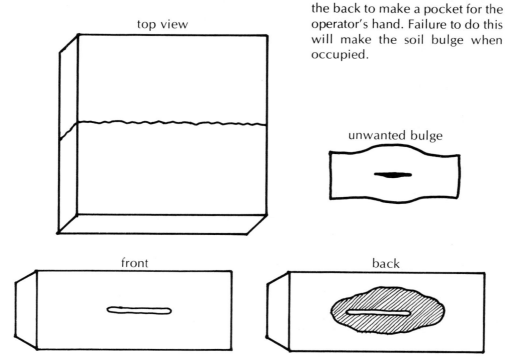

top view

unwanted bulge

front

back

Spray all four soils with brown, quick-drying Varathane paint.

For wayside soil, add thin, black felt eyes that look like slits and appear unhappy. Pin on. Use a dark felt pen to draw a mouth that turns down at the corners.

For rocky soil, make eyes that look like rocks and draw in a sad mouth. Lay real rocks on top.

For thorny soil, add happy eyes and an "al-most-smile." Stick twigs in to represent thorn bushes. Use others in back of the soil when illustrating the growth of the thorns.

For good soil, add a happy face.

A child's red sock makes a wonderful mitt for the puppeteer to wear and use as a tongue.

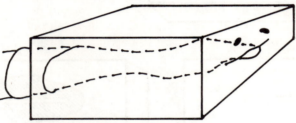

**Two types of soil where the seeds landed.
Foreground: rocky soil; thorny soil is behind it.**

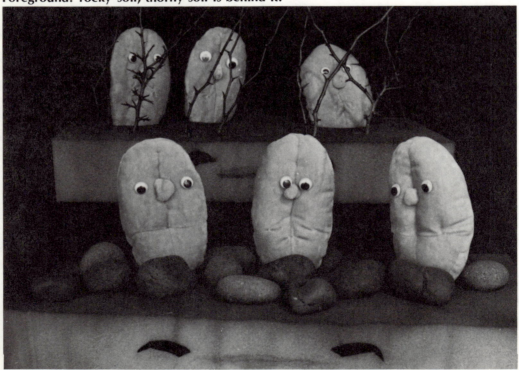

BIRD PATTERN

You will need the following materials:

two pieces of red fake fur (each 9" × 15")
two large red feathers
two movable eyes (3 cm. or 1¼" size)
cardboard (from cereal box or similar thickness)
yellow, orange, and red felt
black embroidery floss
4" styrofoam ball
fabric glue

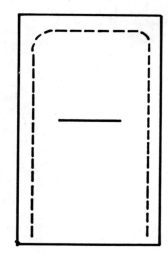

Construction procedure:

Cut a 4" slot for mouth in one piece of fur about eight inches up from the bottom edge. Sew the two sections of fur together, rounding the corners across the top. Leave the bottom open. Turn right side out.

Cut out cardboard diamonds for mouth. Crease top and bottom bills on center fold line. Fold mouth inside. Tape cardboard mouth together, matching letters. Cover top and bottom with yellow felt cut slightly larger than cardboard pattern in order to overlap the edges. Secure with fabric glue. Add orange felt (of the same size as the inside mouth pattern) to inside of mouth. Glue down. Add a red felt tongue. Stitch bill to fur with black floss to make two nostrils (see photo on page 28). Stitch bottom bill to fur. Cover stitching with a long wedge of orange felt. Glue on eyes. Poke feathers in for horns. Stuff with styrofoam or Nerf ball.

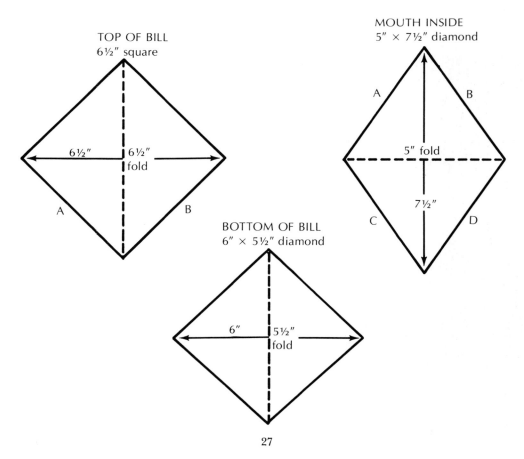

TOP OF BILL
6½" square

6½" 6½"
fold

A   B

MOUTH INSIDE
5" × 7½" diamond

A   B

5" fold

7½"

C   D

BOTTOM OF BILL
6" × 5½" diamond

6" 5½"
fold

Bird that snatched away some seeds.

REPAIRING THE TEMPLE: GOD'S BOOK FOUND

**A five-act puppet play on the life and work of Josiah, king of Judah from
II Kings 22–23, and II Chronicles 34–35.**

Characters:
  Narrator
  King Josiah
  Shaphan—the scribe
  Hilkiah—the high priest
  Ahikam—Shaphan's son
  Achbor—Micah's son
  Asaiah—the king's servant
  Huldah—the prophetess
  Shallum—her husband
  a Carpenter
  a Stonemason
  Two general workmen

Props:
  lumber
  hammer
  stone
  dust bunnies (fleece)
  scraps of cloth
  storage chest
  miniature scroll

Scene One: Palace

Before curtain opens Narrator reads II Kings 22:1–3a. "Josiah was eight years old when he became king, and he reigned thirty-one years in Jerusalem; and his mother's name was Jedidah the daughter of Adaiah of Bozkath. And he did that which was right in the sight of the LORD, and walked in all the way of his [great, great—ever so great grand]* father David, nor did he turn aside to the right or to the left. Now it came to pass in the eighteenth year of King Josiah, that . . ."

(Curtain Opens)

King Josiah:	*(Standing to the right of stage center, calls.)* Servant!
Servant:	*(Enters quickly and bows.)* You called, Your Majesty?
King Josiah:	Yes, send for Shaphan, the scribe. I have work for him to do.
	(Servant leaves. King paces slowly. Servant returns with Shaphan.)
Shaphan:	*(Approaches king and bows.)* You called for me, Your Majesty?
King Josiah:	Yes. Go up to Hilkiah, the high priest at the temple, and have him get that place cleaned up and repaired. There's money in the treasury there. He can pay for carpenters, stonemasons, builders and general cleaning people—whatever he needs. The house of the Lord has been neglected and it's a disgrace. Hire honest men and get the work done quickly. You are the supervisor.

*Insert this to help explain the relationship to King David.

29

Shaphan:	(*Bowing.*) Yes, Your Majesty.
King Josiah:	Any questions?
Shaphan:	No, Your Majesty.
King Josiah:	Then go.
Shaphan:	Yes, Your Majesty. (*Bows and quickly backs away, leaving quickly*).

(Curtain)

Scene Two: Temple

The workmen are busy cleaning up. Shaphan stands at stage right, supervising. Carpenter goes past with hammer and board, stonemason goes by carrying stone block (made of sponge, styrofoam, or light stone), general workers may be sweeping. Hilkiah digs through an old storage box.)

While they work, they sing:

Clean-ing up the tem-ple,

Clean-ing up the tem-ple,

Clean-ing up the tem-ple of the Lord.

Breth-ren, won't you help us? Chil-dren, won't you help us?

Clean-ing up the tem-ple of the Lord!

	(*Puppets sing through song two or three times while they keep time to the music. The carpenter and stonemason come and go across stage. Others continue cleaning. Toss up giant size dust bunnies. When puppets begin singing the song through again, stop with "Cleaning up the temple, cleaning up the temple, cleaning up . . .")*
Hilkiah:	"Shaphan!" (*Silence, puppets freeze.*) Look! (*Puppets look. Hilkiah walks toward Shaphan.*) I have found the book of the law in the house of the Lord! (*Holds up book.*)
Everybody:	The book of the law?
Hilkiah:	(*Emphatically.*) The book of the law!
Everybody:	In the house of the Lord?
Hilkiah:	(*Emphatically.*) Yes. In the house of the Lord!
Shaphan:	May I see it? (*Hilkiah hands it to Shaphan, who unrolls it and begins to read.*) "And you shall again obey the LORD, and observe all His commandments. . . . "See, I have set before you this day life and good, and death and evil. If you obey the commandments of the LORD your God which I command you this day, by loving the LORD your God, by walking in his ways, and by keeping his commandments and his statutes and ordinances, then you shall live and multiply, and the LORD thy God will bless you in the land which you goest to take possession of it. But if thine heart turn away so that wilt not hear, but shalt be drawn away to worship other gods, and serve them, I denounce unto you this day, that you shall live long upon the land which you are going over the Jordan to enter and possess. I call heaven and earth to witness against you this day, that I have set before you life and death, blessing and curse, therefore choose life, that you and your descendants, by loving the LORD your God, by obeying his voice, and cleaving to him; for that means life to you and length of days, that you may dwell in the land which the LORD swore to your fathers, to Abraham, to Isaac, and to Jacob, to give them."* (*Shaphan stops, looks up.*) . . . His Majesty, King Josiah, should know about this right away. I'll take it to him. (*Exits.*)

(*Curtain*)

Scene Three: Palace

King Josiah is on stage. Servant enters from left stage after curtain opens.

Servant:	(*Bowing.*) Your Majesty, Shaphan, the scribe, is here to see you.

*Note: Scripture verses are from Deuteronomy 30:8, 15–20, RSV.

King Josiah:	Good, send him in.
	(*Servant exits.*)
Shaphan:	(*Enters from left stage, bows before King.*) Your Majesty, your servants have emptied out the money that was in the treasury and have paid good workmen who are repairing and cleaning the house of the Lord.
King Josiah:	Good, then the work is progressing on schedule?
Shaphan:	Yes, Your Majesty. And . . . and Hilkiah the priest has given me a book. (*Holds up the scroll for King Josiah to see.*)
King Josiah:	What book is it?
Shaphan:	With Your Majesty's permission, I would like to read some of this book. It's God's book. (*Begins to read.*)
	Hear, O Israel: The LORD is our God, the LORD is one! And you shall love the LORD your God with all your heart, and with all your soul, and with all your might. And these words which I command you this day, shall be upon your heart; and you shall teach them diligently to your children, and shall talk of them when you sit in your house, and when you walk by the way and when you lie down and when you rise. And you shall bind them as a sign upon your hand, and they shall be as frontlets between your eyes.
	And you shall write them on the doorposts of your house and on your gates.
	And when the LORD your God brings you into the land which He swore to your fathers, to Abraham, to Isaac, and to Jacob, to give you, great and goodly cities, which you did not build, and houses full of all good things which you did not fill, and cisterns hewn out, which you did not hew, and vineyards and olive trees which you did not plant, and when you eat and are full, then, take heed, lest you forget the LORD who brought you out of the land of Egypt, out of the house of bondage. You shall fear the LORD your God; and you shall serve him, and swear by his name. You shall not go after other gods, of the gods of the peoples who are round about you; for the LORD your God in the midst of you is a jealous God; lest the anger of the LORD your God be kindled against you, and he destroy you from off the face of the earth."*
King Josiah:	That is God speaking through His book. It has been lost all this time. Our people have not been obeying His Word. They don't know about God because they are not taught. Our land is full of idols. We will be wiped off the face of the earth.
	(*Shaphan bows sadly.*)
King Josiah:	Oh, Lord, forgive me! I didn't know. (*Tears his clothes and mourns.*)
	(*Shaphan backs out, bowing as he goes, toward left stage exit.*)
King Josiah:	(*Calls.*) Shaphan, you and Hilkiah, the high priest, and Ahikam, your son, and Achbor, Micah's son, and Asaiah, my servant, have an important errand to do for me.
	(*Shaphan comes back for orders.*)
Shaphan:	Yes, Your Majesty?
King Josiah:	I want all of you to go to Shallum's home. He's the keeper of the wardrobe. He lives on the other side of the city. Talk to his wife,

*Note: Scripture verses are from Deuteronomy 6:4–15 RSV.

Huldah. She is a prophetess and should be able to tell us what God is going to do to us now, for our fathers have not listened to the words of this Book. Get the men and go quickly. It's urgent!

Shaphan: *(Bows and replies as he exits.)*
We will go immediately, Your Majesty.
(Curtain)

Scene Four: Huldah's home

Men approach the door. Asaiah knocks.
Door is opened by Shallum.

Shallum: Yes?

Asaiah: Shallum, the keeper of the wardrobe?

Shallum: Yes, I am Shallum. What do you want?

Asaiah: We have a message from His Majesty, King Josiah. *(Asaiah steps aside and Shaphan moves up to address Shallum.)*

Shaphan: King Josiah has sent us to see your wife.

Shallum: To see my wife? All of you?

Shaphan: Yes. This is Hilkiah, the high priest *(They bow to one another in greeting as they are introduced.)*, Ahikam, my son *(Both bow.)*, Acbor *(Both bow.)*, and Asaiah, the king's servant *(Both bow.)*. I am Shaphan, the scribe *(Both bow.)*.

Shallum: I'll call Huldah. *(To inside.)* Huldah! You have some company. *(To the men.)* I'll send her out. *(He enters house.)*

Huldah: Hello—you must be from the king. *(Shaphan pushes Hilkiah toward Huldah so he can talk to her.)*

Hilkiah: *(Bowing in greeting.)* Huldah, we were sent to you by His Majesty, King Josiah. This is Shaphan *(Both bow.)* his son, Ahikam *(Both bow.)*, Acbor *(Both bow.)*, and Asaiah, the king's servant *(Both bow.)*. I am Hilkiah, the high priest.

Huldah: What can I do for you?

Hilkiah: We understand that you are a prophetess and know God well. Tell us, has He shown His fate of our people? We have found God's Book in the temple, and the king is very worried because people have not kept God's commandments. His Book claims that we will be de-stroyed—wiped off the face of the earth!

Huldah: Thus says the LORD God of Israel, "Tell the man who sent you to me, thus says the LORD, 'Behold, I will bring evil upon this place and upon its inhabitants, all the words of the Book which the king of Judah has read. Because they have forsaken Me and have burned incense to other gods that they might provoke Me to anger with all the work of their hands, therefore my wrath burns against this place,

33

and it shall not be quenched. But to the king of Judah, who sent you to inquire of the LORD, thus shall you say to him, Thus says the LORD the God of Israel: Regarding the words which you have heard, because your heart was penitent, and you humbled yourself before the LORD when you heard how I spoke against this place and against its inhabitants, that they should become a desolation and a curse, and you have torn your clothes and wept before me, I also have heard you,' says the LORD. Therefore, behold, I will gather you to your fathers, and you shall be gathered to your grave in peace, and your eyes shall not see all the evil which I will bring upon this place.'* (*Pause.*)

That is God's message.

(*Huldah turns and reenters her home.*)

Men: We must take this word back to the king. (*Exit.*)

(*Curtain*)

Scene Five: Palace

King Josiah stands in front of his throne giving orders to the men whom he had sent to Huldah.

King Josiah: Hilkiah, you and your men are to destroy the things of Baal that are in the temple. Burn all of them to cinders outside of the city and carry the ashes away. We will no longer serve Baal. (*Hilkiah bows and leaves.*) Shaphan, you and your men are to get rid of all the idolatrous priests in this country—those who worship Baal, those who worship the sun, those who worship the moon, and anyone who worships any constellation of heaven or any of its hosts! (*Shaphan bows and leaves.*)

Achbor, you and your men are to go throughout all this land and get rid of all the altars in high places, and destroy every idol. Grind them to dust. (*Achbor bows and leaves.*)

Ahikam, you and your men get rid of the cult prostitutes, destroy Topeth in the valley—a man may no longer let his son or daughter walk through that fire for the false god, Molech. (*Ahikam bows and leaves.*)

Asaiah, my servant, there are things to do here at the palace and up at the temple. You and the rest of the servants destroy all of the altars that the former kings have put on the rooftops of this very palace, and in the temple. Grind them to powder and dump the dust in the river. And, while you're at it, get rid of all the horses over there by the temple that the sun worshipers have dedicated to their god. (*Asaiah bows.*)

Asaiah: (*As he is leaving.*) Your Majesty, may the Lord God of Heaven bless you for your decision to serve Him only. (*Exits.*)

* Note: Scripture is from II Kings 22:15–20.

King Josiah: Now, as soon as things are cleaned up, I will command that all the people of the country celebrate the Passover of the Lord our God who gave us this land, as it is written in the Book of His covenant. (*Bows his head.*) Thank you, Lord God, for giving us your Holy Word.
(Curtain)

(*Music for "Cleaning Up the Temple" could be played softly or hummed while the Narrator reads this last section.*)

Narrator: "Surely such a Passover had not been celebrated from the days of the judges who judged Israel, nor in all the days of the kings of Israel and of the kings of Judah. . . .

Moreover, Josiah removed the mediums and the spiritists and the teraphim and the idols and all the abominations that were seen in the land of Judah and in Jerusalem, that he might confirm the words of the law which were written in the book that Hilkiah the priest found in the house of the LORD. And before him there was no king like him who turned to the LORD with all his heart and with all his soul and with all his might, according to all the law of Moses; nor did any like him arise after him."*

*Note: Scripture is from II Kings 23:22, 24–25.

Ruth (left) and Naomi.

RUTH: FROM RAGS TO RICHES

A six-act puppet play from the Book of Ruth.

Characters:
Ruth
Naomi
Orpah
Boaz

Props:
vase of flowers
little clay lamp
two bundles of grain
bundle of food
bundle wrapped up to represent baby
signs that read LATER,
 and EARLY THE NEXT MORNING.

Note: The first puppet on the stage is the one with whom an audience identifies. This beginning is most unusual in that there are three characters and all are sad: not a very pleasant situation with which to identify—but, hopefully, it will bring the audience to a happy ending as the viewers realize God's plan is working through Ruth.

Scene One: Poor home

Three women, veiled and dressed in black, are sobbing. Ruth's actions and attitude need to be emphasized a little more than the others.

(Sobbing as curtain opens.)

Naomi: They are gone! Gone! We've lost them all! (Sobs.).

Ruth: Oh, my husband—he's dead! We were so happy together. Why? Why did it happen?

Orpah: My dear husband is dead! (Sobs.)

Naomi: I can't bear it. Oh, my daughters, what shall we do?

Ruth: We need someone to help us.

Orpah: But we don't have a husband or sons.

Naomi: Oh, Lord, you know we are all alone. What shall we do? (All sob and huddle together.)

(Curtain)

Scene Two: Roadside

The three women are still dressed in black, but head veils may be back or they may wear a touch of color, such as a light-colored head scarf.

Naomi: Yes, daughters, I've made up my mind. I'm going back to my old home in the country of Judah. Back to Bethlehem. Perhaps even to the same house.

Orpah: We want to go with you.

Naomi: I've heard that the famine there is over. God has visited the people by giving them food again. It will be better there than here.

Orpah: I want to go with you, Mother Naomi.

Ruth: I'm willing to go, also. Don't ask me to leave you.

Naomi: No, my daughters. It would be good to stay together for we love one another, and we have gone through a lot of sorrow, but this is your homeland, and your people. You should each go back to your mother's house. May God deal kindly with you, as you have dealt with the dead and with me. And may God give you peace in your hearts, and each another husband.
(*They embrace one another, kiss goodbye and weep again.*)

Ruth and Orpah: No! No! We want to go with you to your land and your people.

Naomi: No. Why should you go with me? I will have no more sons to be your husbands. I am too old to even think of marrying again. Even if I did, and could have children, would you wait to marry them when they were grown? No, my daughters. This is harder for me than it is for you. God's hand has gone against me.
(*Ruth and Orpah both cry and hug Naomi again. Orpah steps back, but Ruth still clings to Naomi. Orpah bows head and leaves stage sobbing.*)

Naomi: *Ruth*, your sister-in-law has gone back to her people and her gods, you should go back with her.

Ruth: Do not urge me to leave you or to turn back from following you; for where you go, I will go, and where you lodge, I will lodge. Your people shall be my people, and your God, my God. Where you die, I will die, and there I will be buried. Thus may the Lord do to me, and worse, if anything but death parts you and me.

Naomi: Let's be on our way then. I can see that you have made up your mind—and I'll not change it. (*Exit.*)
(*Curtain*)

Scene Three: Inside home in Bethlehem

Ruth and Naomi are talking inside the old home in Bethlehem.

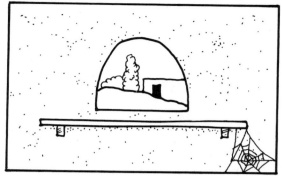

Naomi:	(*Looking around the room.*) Well, this is it, my daughter. I'm home at last. This isn't much to look at now . . . but I do remember when my husband and I had a nice home here in Bethlehem years ago. . . .
Ruth:	God will make us happy again, Mother Naomi. He can do it. I know He can.
Naomi:	(*Reflectively.*) I had a lot when we left here; my husband, my two sons . . . so much! Now everything is gone. (*Pause.*) Some of my husband's family stayed here through the famine years. Perhaps you will get to meet them soon. Well, I must get to work and clean up this house.
Ruth:	We must also think of earning some money for food. It is barley harvest time. Please let me go to the field and glean among the ears of grain after anyone in whose sight I may find favor.
Naomi:	Go, my daughter, but it will be very hard work.
Ruth:	I can do it. I will be back later. (*Exits.*)
Naomi:	(*To herself.*) She is such a blessing to me. I don't know how she can put up with me—a mother-in-law. She is better to me than seven sons. I'm so thankful for her love. May the Lord bless her today, and direct her to a good barley field.

(*Curtain*)

Hold up sign that says:

Scene Four: Same as three

Curtain reopens, home has been cleaned, flowers sit in window or on ledge.

39

Naomi: I wonder where Ruth went? It's getting so late. It's almost dark outside. (*Puts candle on ledge.*) I hope she doesn't get lost on the way home. Surely someone would help her. Everyone in town knows about us already. (*Pause.*) She must be very hungry. There's nothing here for us to eat. Do I hear footsteps? That must be her! (*Hurries toward edge of stage where door would be. Ruth enters with bundle of grain.*) Oh, Ruth, I'm so glad to see you. Where have you been? And what do you have? Come in, daughter, come in. Put down your load. (*Ruth puts load on floor.*)

Ruth: Oh, Mother Naomi—just wait until you hear what happened to me today!

Naomi: Tell me, my daughter. But you must be very hungry. I made something to drink—that's about all we have.

Ruth: I'm not hungry. Look, I got all this barley today.

Naomi: All that in one day! You really worked. No wonder you were gone so long.

Ruth: I'm exhausted! But now we have food to eat and, oh, yes here's some food left from my noon meal. The man gave me so much that I couldn't eat it all, so I brought some of it home for you. (*Ruth takes out little bundle of food and gives it to Naomi.*)

Naomi: (*Takes it and eats.*) What man? What happened to you today?

Ruth: Well, I happened to come to a nice field of barley, and asked the men if I could work there behind the reapers. They said I could. Then later when the owner came by, he talked to me and asked me to have lunch with him. He gave me so much to eat I couldn't finish it all. He asked about you. He knew your family and had heard about me. He told me to work in his fields all summer and not go anywhere else. He was very kind.

Naomi: God was surely with you, Ruth.

Ruth: Yes, Mother Naomi, He was. Even when I was picking up grain it seemed as though the workers in front of me were dropping so much I could barely pick it all up. And when I got thirsty the owner said I could drink from his well.

Naomi: Who is this man that was so kind to you? Do you know his name?

Ruth: His name is Boaz.

Naomi: Boaz! He's one of my husband's relatives.

Ruth: That's why he was kind to me, isn't it? He said, "May the Lord reward your work, and your wages be full from the LORD, the God of Israel, under whose wings you have come to seek refuge."

Naomi: May he be blessed of the Lord who has not withdrawn his kindness to the living nor to the dead. It is good that you have been invited to work with his maidens all summer. That is best. Now we must get some rest.

Ruth: (*Yawns.*) Yes, and tomorrow I'll go again.
(Curtain)

Scene Five: Same setting

Ruth and Naomi are talking.

Naomi: Ruth, now that the summer harvest is over, you can rest.

Ruth: Yes, for a while, but I'll get another job.

Naomi: It would be good if you didn't have to work so hard anymore.

Ruth: I don't mind working. We need the food. And I love you and I want to help.

Naomi: You've helped me so much, Ruth. Now, I think there is something I can do for you. Boaz is a good man.

Ruth: Yes, (*Smiling.*) yes he is.

Naomi: Good, I'm glad you like him because I have a plan that involves you and him.

Ruth: You do?

Naomi: Listen carefully, my daughter. Tonight Boaz will be winnowing the grain on the threshing floor. Get washed up, put on your perfume and your best clothes, and go down to the threshing floor, but do not let anyone see you.
After he has finished, and has had something to eat and drink, he will lie down to sleep. When he has fallen asleep, very quietly go up to him and uncover his feet. When they get cold in the middle of the night he will wake up and discover you there at his feet. Then he will tell you what to do.

Ruth: I will do all that you say.

Naomi: Then hurry and get ready. It's going to be dark soon.
(*Ruth leaves stage to left, Naomi leave to right.*) Do not draw curtain, but move sign across stage that says:

EARLY THE NEXT MORNING...

Naomi: (*Enters—yawning and stretching.*) I wonder how Ruth is doing? She will probably come home soon. I can hardly wait. (*Paces floor.*) Oh, here she comes now. (*Ruth enters.*) Come in. Tell me ... what happened?

41

Ruth:	Oh, Naomi, it was exciting. I was afraid I'd get caught, but no one saw me. I was too excited to sleep. He finally discovered me. It really surprised him! We talked a lot last night. Then he gave me this grain to bring home. Today he plans to find a redeemer for me.
Naomi:	Just wait patiently, my daughter. Everything will work out. I can assure you that Boaz will not rest today until he has found the right redeemer, and . . . I have a feeling that I know who it will be.
Ruth:	So do I (*Happy sigh*.).

(*Curtain*)

Scene Six: Interior of fancy home

A year later Ruth, Naomi, and Boaz are talking. Naomi is holding baby (bundle wrapped up).

Boaz:	(*Pleased*.) We've just ended another barley harvest.
Ruth:	(*Teasing*.) And I didn't even get to work in the fields with you.
Boaz:	You were busy planning for the baby.
Ruth:	Yes, I love caring for our little baby, Obed.
Naomi:	And I love being a grandmother to him.
Boaz:	And I love all of you.

(*Curtain*)

ELIJAH FLEES FROM JEZEBEL

A six-act puppet play from I Kings 18 and 19.

Characters:
Elijah
Servant
Jezebel
Angel
Voice
Narrator

Props:
letter
juniper tree
loaf of bread
jar, noise-makers
sign: LATER
brush or grass for broom
rocks, cellophane
imitation flames

Scene One: Inside a home

Elijah and his servant are reviewing the events of the day.

Elijah:	Well, my servant. It's been quite a day! We've truly seen the power of our God!
Servant:	It's good to be alive!
Elijah:	What did you think of the challenge we had with the prophets of Baal?
Servant:	It was great, Master Elijah. Just great.
Elijah:	Jezebel's priests of Baal tried everything to arouse their god.
Servant:	Do you think they truly believed Baal would answer them by burning their offering?
Elijah:	Yes, they did. Otherwise they wouldn't have been so frenzied and cut themselves and leaped on the altar. They lost all sense of reason after awhile. They were desperate.
Servant:	(*Sadly.*) They were. They must have known that failure meant death.
Elijah:	Failure for us would have meant death too. Aren't you thankful that we work on the team for the living God.
Servant:	Yes. Just to watch the fire from heaven fall on that water-soaked sacrifice yesterday afternoon gave me goosebumps all over.
Elijah:	When God does something He does it right.
Servant:	Even the rainstorm last night that ended the drought was fantastic.
Elijah:	God sent a downpour. Just like He said He would.
Servant:	Praise the Lord. God cares for us.

Elijah:	He certainly does! (*Weary sigh.*) I'm exhausted.
Servant:	No wonder! You've been through a lot. And your race outrunning the king's chariot was something else.
Elijah:	Yes. I guess it was. God gave me strength for that, too. Well, let's get some rest. (*Yawn.*)
Servant:	Good idea. (*Yawn.*) (*They both nod and fall asleep.*)
	(*Curtain*)

Scene Two: Jezebel's room in palace

Jezebel has discovered the ill fate of her servants of Baal.

Jezebel: (*Screams of anger.*) How could he do this to me? That hateful Elijah. I despise him! He will have to pay dearly for what he has done! Killed all my prophets! Oh, my god, Baal. What shall I do now? I am ruined. Ruined. (*Pause.*) I will get even. I'll have Elijah killed just like he had them killed. He'll get the message of his life. The last message of his life. (*She gets a paper and writes.*)*

To Elijah:
   So may the gods do to me and even more, if I do not make your life as the life of one of them by tomorrow about this time.
                                                                 Queen Jezebel

(*Happily.*) Now to send a messenger to Elijah's place with this. Servant! Bring me a good messenger—one who can make it through this rainstorm to Elijah's place. Have I got news for him. (*Jezebel laughs wickedly. Servant exits.*)

Scene Three: Same as Scene One

Elijah and his servant are sleeping when there is a knock. (See preceding note.) They rouse, mumbling, settle down again. Knock comes again.

*Note: This was probably sent as a verbal message rather than a written one, so if you would like to use a puppet as a verbal messenger for Jezebel, add him to the script here and also at the beginning of Scene 3.

Messenger's Voice: *(Calling.)* A message for Elijah. Are you there?

Elijah: *(Mumbling sleepily.)* You'd better get the door.

Servant: *(Sleepily.)* Yes, master.
(Servant goes to the door and gets letter.)

Elijah: What is the message that you have received? You look worried.

Servant: Master, listen to this. *(Reads.)* "You have killed my prophets! So may the gods do to me and even more, if I do not make your life as the life of one of them by tomorrow about this time." It's signed, Queen Jezebel.

Elijah: Let me see that! *(He takes the letter and reads it aloud.)* "So may the gods do to me and even more, if I do not make your life as the life of one of them by tomorrow about this time."

Servant: That's no idle threat. She knows where you are because her messenger found you.

Elijah: That's right. She knows exactly where we are. C'mon, let's go. *(They both rush out.)*

Scene Four: *(optional)*

Include this for effect. If you want to omit it, alter the beginning of the next scene to let people know that Elijah has left his servant behind in Beersheba.

Elijah and his servant are running: make running movements near center stage, Elijah is always in the lead.

Keep them running in place and move the backdrop to give the effect of scenery going past.

Use circular track for the backdrop or pin it to the edge of a big umbrella and rotate it slowly. The same scenery can pass by several times.

Servant:	Master, how far are we going?
Elijah:	As far away as we can get.
Servant:	But we could hide nearby.
Elijah:	Jezebel will not give up that easily. One of her soldiers would find us for sure.
Servant:	We've been walking for hours. Can't we stop and rest? I'm exhausted.
Elijah:	Just for a minute. (*They stop and moving background stops.*)
Servant:	I think we could get lost here in Beersheba. I doubt if Jezebel would send soldiers to search here. It's too far from Samaria.
Elijah:	I'm not stopping. But you may if you like. Don't tell anyone who you are and don't tell people that you work for me. I'm going on.
Servant:	Master, are we really parting? You would leave me?
Elijah:	We have no choice. You can't go on and I can't stay. We must separate for now. When it is safe—and who knows when that will be—I'll come look for you in the market street of Beersheba. We will find one another again if God wills. Farewell, my faithful servant. (*They embrace.*)
Servant:	Farewell, master, may God keep us both safe. (*Servant leaves to the right of stage. Elijah begins walking again.*)
Elijah:	I must find a place to rest soon. If I can just make it for another day, I'll be in the wilderness. They will never think to look for me there. I've never been more discouraged in my whole life! Not one friend left on earth. Oh, God, what am I going to do? (*Curtain*)

Scene Five: Desert with juniper tree in foreground

Scene opens as Elijah enters, and plops down under the juniper tree.

Elijah:	Ahhh, some shade at last! I can't go any further. I didn't realize this desert was so hot and barren. I've got to rest. I hope I'll be safe here. Oh, my God, just let me die here! Take my life, for I'm no better than my fathers. (*Lies down and falls asleep.*)
Angel:	(*Comes on stage with cake of bread and a jar of water; puts them down. Taps Elijah on the shoulder.*) Wake up! Get up and eat! (*Exits.*)

(Elijah rouses himself, looks around, sees food, eats without talking and falls asleep again.)

Hold up sign that says:

Angel:	*(Comes again with more food, places it on ledge, then touches Elijah on the shoulder again.)* Arise, eat, else the journey is too great for you. *(Exits.)*
Elijah:	*(Rouses himself, looks around, mumbling.)* I thought I heard someone talking but I don't see anyone. Food. God must have sent it. It's a miracle. I thought I was dreaming before, but maybe God did send an angel to bring me food. Thank you, Lord, for giving me something to eat and drink! *(He eats.)* This is the greatest food I've ever tasted. I feel stronger already. I will go up to Mt. Horeb, the mountain of God.

(Curtain)

Scene Six: Cave

Elijah enters the stage, sees a cave, begins to explore it.

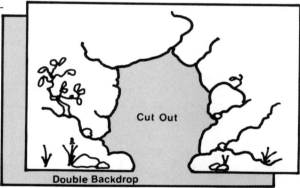

Elijah:	This cave may be just the hideaway I need. I'm going to set up my home here. I should be safe. *(Gets some brushy twigs or grass and sweeps it out, then settles down in entranceway.)*
Voice:	What are you doing here, Elijah?
Elijah:	*(Jumps up and looks all around.)* I have been very zealous for the LORD, the God of hosts; for the sons of Israel have forsaken Thy covenant, torn down Thine altars and killed Thy prophets with the sword. And I alone am left; and they seek my life, to take it away.
Voice:	Go forth, and stand on the mountain before the Lord. *(Elijah moves forward. Sound of wind comes; things blow past. Use a hairdryer or vacuum hose. Bang some rocks together, snap some styrofoam or plastic cartons. Wind and noise subside and all becomes quiet.)*
Elijah:	How frightening. God did not speak to me in the wind. *(Elijah goes back into entranceway and sits down. An earthquake comes.)*

Elijah:	(*Jumps up.*) An earthquake. How dreadful! The earth is shaking. Oh, my God, are you here? (*Shakily moves outside entrance of cave again, anticipating.*) (*Cave entrance vibrates. Earthquake rumbles — snap twigs. Noise dies down. Movement of cave entrance ceases.*)
Elijah:	Ohhhh, it's over! But God was not in the earthquake. Where are you, Lord? Speak to me. (*Waits expectantly; goes back and sits down in cave entrance. Crackle cellophane paper to make noise for fire.*)
Elijah:	(*Jumps up.*) Now what! A fire! A forest fire! And the flames are coming right up the mountain to my cave. I can't escape. What shall I do? (*Backs into cave.*)

(*Flames gradually come up into view at front of stage. See illustration. Flames quiver and then gradually go back down.*)

Elijah:	Oh, God, surely you are in the fire! You were in the fire on the altar at Mt. Carmel. Speak to me, God. Take away my fear. (*A gentle noise of blowing begins.*) (*Elijah wraps his mantle around his face and comes out to cave entrance again.*)
Voice:	What are you doing here, Elijah?
Elijah:	I have been very zealous for the LORD, the God of hosts, for the sons of Israel have forsaken Thy covenant, torn down Thine altars and killed Thy prophets with the sword. And I alone am left; and they seek my life, to take it away.
Voice:	Go, return on your way. You still have work to do for me. Cheer up! I have 7,000 people in Israel who have not bowed their knees to Baal nor kissed him. You are not alone, and I, the LORD your God will always be with you.

(Curtain)

Narrator:	Elijah did not have a dull life. Even though he had days when he got very discouraged—like each of us—God did not leave him nor forsake him. Later, God took Elijah to heaven in a chariot of fire. His follower saw him go up to heaven. When you work for God, you will never be forsaken by Him. Even in very difficult times God will be there to make those times a great blessing. Do you know the Lord? Is your life exciting because you live it for God? Would you like to know Him and serve Him? (*Explain way to salvation.*)

OBEDIENCE

A ten-minute presentation of four Old Testament characters and their obedience—or disobedience—to God taken from Exodus 3–4, Esther, Ruth, and 1 Samuel 15.

Characters:
Narrator Puppet (preferably a vent
   figure or other large puppet)
Voice of angel
Moses
Esther
Servant
Ruth
Naomi
Saul
Samuel

Props:
big Bible
burning bush
bright light
walking stick
serpent
message on paper
bundle of grain

Narrator Puppet: (*Comes up behind a draped table or lectern beside stage.*) Oh, boy, what an assignment! Pastor———, wants a puppet show on obedience. Let's see! What characters in the Bible were obedient? . . . Hmmm, gotta think (*Scratches head.*). Ahh, better start at beginning . . . Genesis . . . Adam and Eve, ah! There we are—the perfect couple. (*Pause.*) Nope! They didn't obey; can't use them.
Well . . . let's see . . . hmmm . . .
What comes next? Uh . . . I'd better get the Bible. (*Goes down and comes up with big Bible. Starts leafing through.*)
Genesis, Exodus—Moses! Let's see what it says about him. Moses is well-known—surely he was obedient.

Narrator Puppet: (*Begins reading.*) Now Moses was pasturing the flock of Jethro his father-in-law, the priest of Midian; and he led the flock to the west-side of the wilderness and came to Horeb, the mountain of God. (*Music begins softly, gradually crescendoing.*)
And the angel of the Lord appeared to him in a blazing fire from the midst of a bush; and he looked, and, behold, the bush was burning with fire, and the bush was not consumed. So Moses said . . .
(*Voice fades off as Narrator puppet looks toward stage.*)

Scene One: Mt. Horeb

Moses comes across bush with artificial, paper flame.

Moses:	What is this? I must turn aside now, and see this marvelous sight, why the bush is not burned up. (*Moses moves closer.*) (*A bright light representing the angel of the Lord appears.*)
Voice:	Moses. Moses!
Moses:	(*Trembling.*) Here I am.
Voice:	Do not come near here. Remove your sandals from your feet, for the place on which you are standing is holy ground. I am the God of your father, the God of Abraham, the God of Isaac, and the God of Jacob. (*Moses hides his face.*)
Voice:	I have surely seen the affliction of My people who are in Egypt, and have heard their cry by reason of their taskmasters; for I am aware of their sufferings. So I am come down to deliver them out of the hand of the Egyptians, and to bring them up out of that land unto a good land and a large land, unto a land flowing with milk and honey. . . . Come now, and I will send thee to Pharoah, so that thou mayest bring forth the children of Israel, out of Egypt. . . . Certainly I will be with thee; and this shall be a sign unto thee, that I have sent thee: When thou hast brought forth the people out of Egypt, ye shall serve God upon this mountain.
Moses:	Behold, when I go to the sons of Israel, and say to them, "The God of your fathers has sent me to you," they may say to me, "What is his Name?" What shall I say to them?
Voice:	I AM WHO I AM. Thus you shall say to the sons of Israel. I AM has sent me to you. . . . This is my name forever. Go to the king of Egypt and say, the Lord God has said let the Hebrew people go a three-days' journey into the wilderness that they may sacrifice to the Lord God.
Moses:	What if they don't believe me when I say the Lord has appeared to me?
Voice:	What is that in your hand?
Moses:	A rod.
Voice:	Throw it on the ground. (*Moses does so and the rod becomes a serpent. Stick goes off backstage and rubber snake appears in its place. Hold with wire. Moses runs away.*)
Voice:	Moses! Come back! Reach out your hand and pick it up by the tail. (*Moses picks it up. The snake becomes a rod again.*)
Voice:	Do this that they may believe the Lord God of your fathers has appeared to you.
Moses:	Please, Lord, I have never been eloquent, neither recently nor in time past, nor since thou hast spoken to Thy servant, for I am slow of speech and slow of tongue.
Voice:	Who has made man's mouth? Who makes him dumb or deaf, or seeing or blind? Is it not I, the LORD? Now then go, and I even I will be with your mouth, and teach you what you are to say.
Moses:	Please, Lord, now send the message by whomever Thou wilt.

Voice:	(*Angry.*) Is there not your brother, Aaron? He shall speak for you to the people.
Moses:	Yes, Lord.

(Curtain)

Narrator Puppet:	(*Speaks from behind table or lectern.*) Boy! I thought he would be a good example of obedience. He was sure reluctant, but . . . he did go and he did obey God. Maybe there's someone else. (*Thumbs through the Bible.*) Here's one—Esther. (*Voice fades as he looks toward puppet stage.*)

Scene Two: *Palace*

Servant:	(*Approaches Queen Esther, bows.*) Your Majesty, Queen Esther. I bring you this message from the servant at the palace gate. (*Hands message to Esther, bows and backs off stage.*)
Esther:	(*Opens message.*) Here's a letter from Cousin Mordecai, the keeper at the palace gate. I wonder if he has advice for me in this time of trouble?
Esther:	I am so afraid we will all be killed. Dear Mordecai has been ever so kind to me—just like a father. (*Reads.*) "Do not imagine that you in the king's palace can escape any more than all the Jews. For if you remain silent at this time, relief and deliverance will arise for the Jews from another place and you and your father's house will perish. And who knows whether you have not attained royalty for such a time as this." What shall I do? I must do something to help save my people. (*Pause.*) I will fast and pray. And the people will all fast and pray. God will help us. I'll answer Cousin Mordecai right away. He can get a message to all the Jews to fast and pray for three days. Then I will go in to the King,—which is not according to the law;—and if I perish, I perish. (*Exits.*)

(Curtain)

Narrator Puppet:	Esther obeyed. And God spared her people, Uh . . . let's see. (*Pause. Looks through Bible.*) Oh, yes, there's Ruth. She obeyed. (*Looks toward puppet stage.*)

Scene Three: Naomi's home

(*Ruth walks in and puts down grain.*)

Naomi:	My daughter, you have been such a blessing to me in my old age. Tell me, what did Boaz say to you?

Ruth: (*Stammers.*) He . . . I, uh . . . he said he was going to visit a kinsman and arrange . . .

Naomi: Don't worry. He won't rest until he has settled the matter. He loves you.

Ruth: Oh, I hope so. But . . . but how do you know?

Naomi: Boaz is a kind man. And wise. He has shown many favors to you since you started working for him. He sent you back with grain this morning. He knows that you have been kind to me, your poor old mother-in-law.

Ruth: (*Interrupts.*) Oh, Naomi—I love you.

Naomi: (*Continuing.*) You have obeyed in every way. That's the kind of woman Boaz would want for a wife. He will come for you. Never fear.

(Curtain)

Narrator Puppet: That's a neat love story . . . and it all happened because Ruth obeyed Naomi and God.
Let's see if I can find one final illustration for Pastor———. (*Thumbs through Bible.*)
Oh, here's one! Saul. King Saul. He started out in his life as a very humble person who wanted to serve God more than anything. What happened in this book?
(*Narrator looks toward puppet stage.*)

Scene Four: Field

Saul: I wonder what has been keeping Samuel, the priest, for so long?
(*Sheep bleat softly at the end of each sentence. The bleating reflects how they feel about each statement.*) I surely thought he would be here before this. We won the battle. I know, God's priest said we were supposed to destroy everything the enemy owned, but . . . but it was stupid to do that, so we saved the best. They will make good sacrifices. Is Samuel coming now? Yes, I think so.
(*Samuel enters.*) Blessed are you of the Lord. I have carried out the commands of the Lord.

Samuel: You have obeyed? Then what is this bleating of the sheep in my ears, and the lowing of the oxen which I hear?

Saul: They have been brought from the enemy camp, for the people spared the best of the sheep and oxen to sacrifice to the Lord your God, but the rest we have utterly destroyed.

Samuel: Wait, let me tell you what the Lord said to me last night.

Saul: Speak!

Samuel: Is it not true, though you were little in your own eyes, that you were made the head of the tribes of Israel? And the LORD anointed you

king over Israel, and the LORD sent you on a mission . . . [to] destroy the sinners, the Amalekites . . . until they were completely exterminated. Why then did you not obey the voice of the Lord, but rushed upon the spoil and did what was evil in the sight of the Lord?

Saul: I did obey the voice of the Lord, and went on the mission on which the Lord sent me, and have brought back Agag the king of Amalek, and have utterly destroyed the Amalekites. But the people took some of the spoil, sheep and oxen, the choicest of the things devoted to destruction, to sacrifice to the Lord your God at Gilgal.

Samuel: Has the Lord as much delight in burnt offerings and sacrifices as in obeying the voice of the Lord? (*Saul hangs his head*.)
Behold, to obey is better than sacrifice, and to heed than the fat of rams. For rebellion is as the sin of [witchcraft] and [disobedience] is as iniquity and idolatry. Because you have rejected the word of the Lord, he has also rejected you from being king.

Saul: I have sinned, I have indeed transgressed the command of the Lord and your words, because I feared the people and listened to their voice. Now therefore, please pardon my sin and return with me, that I may worship the Lord.

Samuel: I will not return with you, for you have rejected the word of the Lord, and the Lord has rejected you from being king over Israel. (*Samuel turns to go. Saul grabs his robe and tears it. An extra section of robe may be fastened on with velcro—it will make a good tearing sound when it is pulled off*.)

Esther, Moses, Samuel, and Saul.

Samuel: The Lord has torn the kingdom of Israel from you today, and has given it to your neighbor who is better than you. And also the Glory of Israel will not lie or change His mind; for He is not a man that He should change His mind.

Saul: (*Kneels before Samuel.*) I have sinned; but please honor me now before the elders of my people and before Israel, and go back with me, that I may worship the Lord your God. (*Sobs.*)

(*Curtain*)

Narrator Puppet: Sadly, Samuel did not see Saul again until the day of his death. Saul did not obey God. Therefore, he spent the rest of his days as a miserable man. It is very important to obey God.

Application

This play may be followed effectively by a short dialogue between the Narrator Puppet and a pastor or leader. Stress one of the following points:

1. To be happy in our lives we should be willing to obey God. We should obey those He has put in authority over us.
2. To know what God expects of us, we should study His word and obey it.
3. To be used of God, we must be obedient to Him in all areas.

Children could also name other Biblical characters who obeyed or disobeyed God.

ZACCHAEUS

A three-act puppet play.

Characters:
  Zacchaeus
  Crowd of 10-15 (enough puppets to
    fill a row across stage)
  Jesus' voice
  Narrator

Props:
  fork holder
  tree
  book or scroll
  coins

Scene One: Ornate home interior

Zacchaeus busily checks over his books and counts his money.

Zacchaeus: One thousand thirty-seven, one thousand thirty-eight, one thousand thirty-nine, one thousand forty. (*Weary sigh*.) Let's see. What do I have recorded for this next person. (*Looks in book, runs finger along list of names*.) Oh, yes, here he is. Joseph Ben Ammond: two thousand five hundred. Hmmmmm. According to my records, I can surely ask him to pay more taxes. He can afford to make quite a substantial boost to my income. Then I can buy those Persian rugs I've been wanting for my walls. Good.

(*Rubs hands together greedily*.) Hmmmm. Let's see. Here's one: Abdul Ben Hadadah. How much is recorded for him? Um, yes! Yes, he can certainly pay more this time. A rich trader like him. He shouldn't complain. He gets to see a lot of the world while I'm stuck here collecting money all the time. Let's see (*Looks through lists again*.) Here's one. Oh, brother, another one of those fisherman. Ben Zebedee. They never like to pay anything. But I can charge him plenty. He had a good fishing season this year. I've seen his fish in the markets. He won't dare complain or I'll charge higher taxes on those marketplaces. Yep! I've got 'em and they know it. They can't outsmart old Zac.

Ho hum. (*Zaccheaus sighs and closes book. Begins counting money again*.) One thousand forty-one, one thousand forty-two, one thousand forty—(*Voice begins to fade. Head nods, jerks himself awake*.) Where was I? Oh, yes, forty thousand one, forty thousand two—is that right? Oh, it doesn't matter anyway. I've counted it so much already. (*Sigh*.) Guess if I had someone to talk to I wouldn't be so bored. All I do is count money and plan to make more. I really would like to have friends but the people in this town don't treat me well because they don't like paying taxes. And I don't like them anyway. (*Changes tone.*) But I still get lonesome. Nothing to do. Guess I'll take a nap. (*Puts head down over books and money. Noise begins outside.*)

Voices: He's coming! He's coming this way! Today? Yes, he will be here. Tell everyone you see. I'm going to get a good place along the street so I can be sure to see him.
(*Loudly.*) Who's coming? (*Zacchaeus raises his head quickly.*).
Jesus, of course. Jesus, of Nazareth, the teacher and prophet of Israel. Some say He is the Messiah we have been looking for.
Maybe He can heal me. I want to hear what He has to say. Let's go.
(*Voices and crowd fade away.*)

Zacchaeus: (*Wide awake.*) Jesus of Nazareth is coming to Jericho? Now? Oh, I want to see him, too.

(*Curtain*)

Scene Two: A city street

Crowd is all lined up, waiting to see Jesus.
(Puppets are on "forks" facing audience.)
A sycamore tree stands behind crowd.

Stage set up as audience will see it.

56

Zacchaeus:	(*Crowd murmurs in anticipation, but Zacchaeus can be heard above them.*) Where's a place for me? (*Tries to get through, but the crowd closes gap on him*). Let me see, too. (*Tries another place, but can't get through.*) Maybe I can get through here. (*Repeat similar tries several times.*) I'll try this place again. (*Doesn't work.*) I must get through. What can I do? I know. Nobody's watching. I'll climb this sycamore tree. No one will notice me up there, and I'll be able to see. (*Zacchaeus climbs up backside so puppeteers arm is hidden, only Zacchaeus's hands show.*) There! Now, I've fooled this stupid group. They'll never know. (*Crowd grows silent.*) 

Voice:	(*Reverently.*) Here he comes. (*Silence.*) He's stopping here.
Zacchaeus:	Oh, no. I think He's seen me. Yes, yes He has. Oh, He is the most wonderful person I have ever seen. His face, and especially His eyes, are so kind. He is looking right at me. He likes me. I know it. Oh, if only we were friends.
Jesus' Voice:	Zacchaeus
Zacchaeus:	He called me by name! How does He know my name?
Jesus' Voice:	Hurry and come down, for today I am staying at your house.
Zacchaeus:	My house? My house? (*Starts down quickly. Crowd parts to let him through.*) Yes, please come to my house. (*Crowd grumbles and mumbles.*)
Voice:	He is going to be the guest of Zacchaeus—a real sinner.
Zacchaeus:	(*Stops and looks out and up. Speaking to Jesus.*) Lord, behold Lord, half of my possessions I will give to the poor, and if I have defrauded anyone of anything, I will give back four times as much.
Jesus' Voice:	Zacchaeus, today salvation has come to this house, . . . For the Son of Man has come to seek and to save that which was lost. (*Zacchaeus walks off to left. Crowd backs up a little.*)
	(*Curtain*)

Scene Three: Zacchaeus' home

Zacchaeus checks his books and counts his money.

Zacchaeus: One thousand forty-five, one thousand forty-six, one thousand forty-seven. There! I can give all this to the poor, and more. Let's see. (*Looks in his book.*) Here'a a name I've checked: Ben Zebedee. I'm going to see him and give him four times whatever I took from him. He'll be so surprised he'll drop his fish all over the place. Really, he's not nearly as bad as I imagined. In fact, he's pretty well-respected around here. I'm sure we can become good friends.
(*Stops to reflect.*) I'm so glad Jesus came to Jericho. I'm so glad I saw Him. I'm so glad He saw me! My life has changed.

(*Curtain*)

Narrator: This is only a puppet play but the story is taken from the Bible. Zacchaeus was a real person who had a need. His need was to accept Christ. He wasn't happy living in his sin and greed. Jesus came and made all the difference. Zacchaeus believed. He straightened out his sin problems with Jesus in front of all the people who despised him. Zacchaeus welcomed Jesus with all his heart. Do you know Jesus? Have you met Him? Jesus died for you. He lives for you. He loves you. And as He called Zacchaeus, He also calls you by your name. He wants to come into your life and take charge—to make you happy and give you eternal life.

HOW TO MAKE A FORK HOLDER FOR A GROUP OF PUPPETS

You will need the following materials:
lightweight strips of wood ¾" - 1" wide
nails or glue
sandpaper
hammer and saw

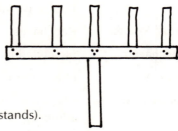

Construction procedure:
Cut woodstrips into 8" lengths for the tines (puppet stands).
Cut an 8" length for the handle
Cut a section for the cross piece allowing three inches per puppet (for example, if you plan to put five puppets on one fork, cut the section 3" × 5" or 15 inches).
Sand the rough spots down.
Fasten the parts together with nails or glue.

Hints for using:
Use uniform heights for bands, armies, or tribes, etc.
but when you want them to vary, try this:
(1) Add an extension with an additional strip and rubber bands.

(2) Shorten by putting a puppet on in front by attaching the neck to a tine with a pipecleaner.

To keep heads from wobbling, stuff the necks with a folded tissue or paper towel.

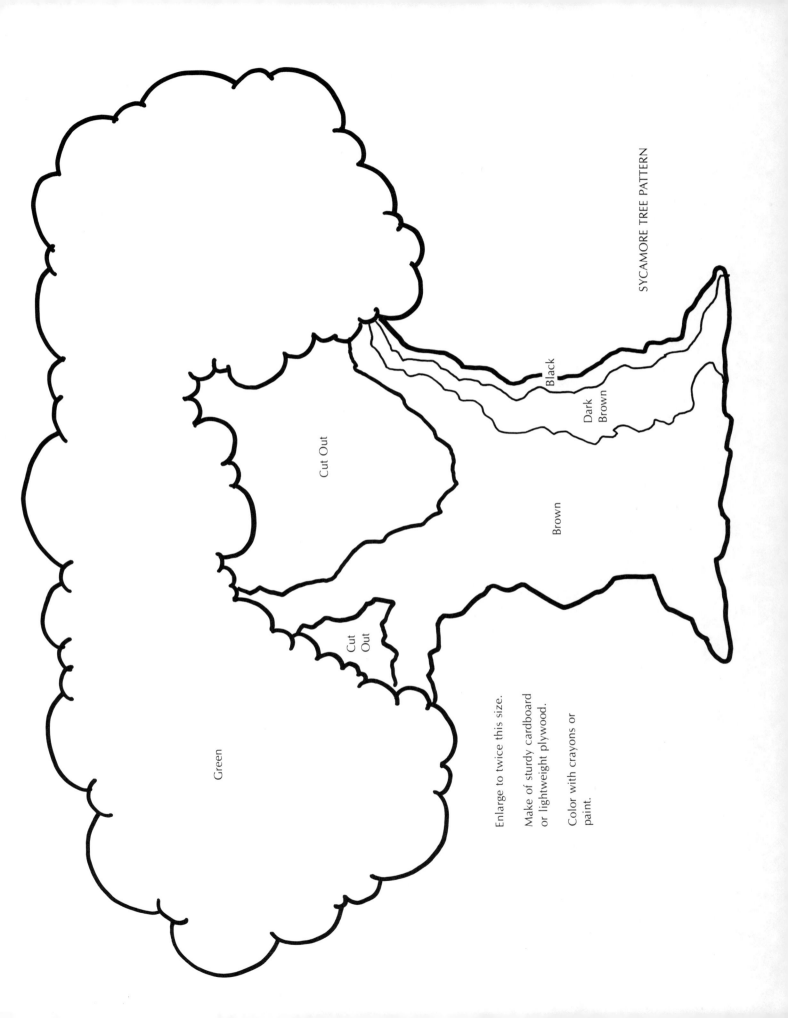

SYCAMORE TREE PATTERN

Black

Dark
Brown

Cut Out

Brown

Cut
Out

Green

Enlarge to twice this size.

Make of sturdy cardboard
or lightweight plywood.

Color with crayons or
paint.

FINDING REAL LOVE ON VALENTINE'S DAY

A one-act puppet play.

Characters:
- Charlie
- Little Girl
- Little Boy
- Girl
- Man & Woman
- Pretty Girl
- Old Lady

Props:
- Valentine box
- cookie hearts
- daisy with detachable petals
- Cupid (cardboard pattern)
- Bible
- chart of John 3:16

Scene One:

Stage is empty. Puppeteer comes out and begins to put up valentine decorations— red & white streamers, hearts, and a cupid.

Charlie:	(*Pops up.*) Hey. What's going on here? What are you doing?
Puppeteer:	Oh, just putting up some decorations.
Charlie:	Decorations for what?
Puppeteer:	For Valentine's Day, Charlie.
Charlie:	Valentine's Day? Never heard of it. What kind of day is that?
Puppeteer:	You've never heard of Valentine's Day?
Charlie:	Nope.
Puppeteer:	Where have you been?
Charlie:	Kept in a box.
Puppeteer:	Oh—I forgot. I'll tell you about it while I finish putting up the decorations. A long time ago there was a man who used to do good deeds. His name was Valentine. People heard about him and of the love he had for the poor. Over the years people tried to show love for others too, especially on his birthday. They called him a saint and that's part of how we got St. Valentine's Day.
Charlie:	Is it like that now—doing good deeds?
Puppeteer:	Well, not really, It's changed a lot. Today people give valentines to those whom they love.
Charlie:	Love?
Puppeteer:	Naturally! Well, I must go now. Bye, Charlie. (*Puppeteer goes back behind stage.*)

Charlie:	Boy, oh, boy, I'm staying right here because I don't want to miss Valentine's Day. Hmmm, the decorations are pretty. I wonder why he put up red hearts? (*Studies decorations.*) And what's this thing that looks like a baby playing with arrows? That could be dangerous. Hey, Buddy (*To Cupid.*) don't shoot me. I'm only looking. (*Little Girl enters stage from left with box of cookies as Charlie watches.*)
Little Girl:	(*Talking to herself.*) I hope Georgie likes the valentine cookies I made him. He's so cute! (*She moves across stage and exits.*)
Charlie:	Valentine cookies?! Never heard of that kind. They looked like sugar cookies to me, only they were shaped like hearts. Hearts? (*Catching on*) There must be something about hearts for Valentine's . . . and I think her heart was kind of sugary. (*Amused.*) Tee Hee! (*Little boy enters from right with a heart-shaped candy box as Charlie watches*).
Little Boy:	(*Talking to himself.*) Oh, Boy! I wonder if Cindy likes me? Wonder if she'll like this valentine candy? I've been saving my allowance since Christmas to get her this. She's so neat (*Sighs*).
Charlie:	Valentine candy?! In that box? And it's the shape of a heart! Now I know what Valentine's Day is! It's when you give somebody you like . . . er . . . love (*laughs*) a heart-shaped cookie or candy. Yippee! (*Begins dancing around.*) (*Another girl enters from right with a big daisy. Charlie stops to watch as she plucks off petals.*)
Girl:	He loves me. He loves me not. He loves me. He loves me not. He loves me. He (*Pulls last petal off.*) loves me! He loves me! (*She waltzes off-stage.*)
Charlie:	What? What was that all about? I thought I had it all figured out, but now . . . Hmmmmm? (*A man and woman walk by. Charlie watches and listens.*)
Man:	I'm glad I found you.
Woman:	I love you, dear.
Man:	I love you too, honey.
Woman:	We've been happy together, haven't we?
Man:	Yes, all these years. Say, what would you like for Valentine's Day?
Woman:	Just you.
Man:	And all I want is you.
Woman:	How sweet! But I'm getting you a little something anyway.
Man:	And I'm getting something for you. (*Exit.*)
Charlie:	Maybe Valentine's Day is more than just giving hearts and cookies and candies and all that! Maybe it's giving nice things to someone you love. Yep, that must be it too. Well, (*Decidedly.*) that doesn't include me. I don't love anybody. Nope, not me. That's a lot of hooey. (*Pretty girl comes on stage from left.*)
Pretty Girl:	(*Sweetly.*) Hi, there.
Charlie:	Oh, . . . uh . . . hi. (*Takes another look.*) I mean Hi! I . . . uh . . . (*Charlie stammers as she goes across stage and exits to right.*) Oh, boy! Was she pretty! I wonder who she is. I want to get acquainted with

	her. But how can I do it? Hmmm, I know. I'll give her a valentine present. Oh, quick, I think she's coming back. What can I get? I know. One of the hearts—the puppeteer won't mind—I can get him another one soon. Oops, she's coming, I gotta hurry. I think she likes me. Oh, I hope, I hope, I hope. (*He reaches up to grab a heart, but he's not watching what he does and he grabs the cupid instead. Quickly he comes down and thrusts it toward her.*)
Charlie:	Hi, I'm Charlie and here's something for you.
Pretty Girl:	Oh, thank you. (*She is pleased until she realizes what he has given her.*) A cupid! Oh, good grief! A cupid! How stupid. (*She drops it and hurries off-stage.*)
Charlie:	Oh, no! (*Calling after her.*) I meant to give you a heart. A heart. (*Pause.*) A cupid? That's a cupid? Maybe she'll come back. Sure (*Trying to convince himself.*), she'll come back! I'll get a heart this time and be ready (*Reaches up and gets a heart.*) Oh, I think I hear her coming. I'll just turn my back to her, then when she's next to me, I'll turn around and really surprise her. (*Gets ready. Old Lady enters.*)
Charlie:	(*Jumps around and shouts:*) Here's my heart. I love you.
Old Lady:	Oh, my goodness! How sweet of you.
Charlie:	(*Realizing his mistake.*) Oh, no—not you! I don't love you! Er . . . I mean, you're not the person I thought you were.
Old Lady:	That's all right, dear. I understand. (*Charlie very bashful, puts his head down, mumbles.*)
Old Lady:	Why don't you ask someone to tell you what *real* love is? Do you know of someone who might help you?
Charlie:	(*Mumbles.*) Mmmmm . . . er . . . I don't know anyone—except maybe the puppeteer who told me all about Valentine's Day. He's smart. Maybe he knows what real love is.
Old Lady:	Good. You ask him. Bye, bye, Sonny. (*Exits.*)
Charlie:	Puppeteer! Puppeteer! (*Looks around as he calls.*) Oh, valentine puppeteer! Where are you?
Puppeteer:	(*Approaches.*) Here I am, Charlie. (*Carries more decorations and a Bible.*) What can I do for you?
Charlie:	What's real love?
Puppeteer:	Real love? Why do you ask? (*Charlie hangs his head in embarrassment.*)
Puppeteer:	Sorry, I didn't mean to embarrass you. I think you've spent too much time in your box. Do you like someone extra special? (*Charlie nods affirmatively.*)
Puppeteer:	Well, it could be that you feel love—or you may be just infatuated.
Charlie:	I'm not sick!
Puppeteer:	No! No! Infatuated doesn't mean you're sick—it just means you have a crush on somebody.
Charlie:	Oh. What's real love?
Puppeteer:	Real love is . . . well, real love is . . . (*Looks down at his handful of streamers and his Bible.*) I know—this should explain it. (*Holds up*

Bible.) Real love is what God feels for each person. He loves us all, even though we aren't perfect. He loves us so much that He let His Son die in our place. He wants each person to live with Him forever. He gave people the Bible so they could share that message. That's real love. Loving someone so much that one will give everything for the good of that person.

Charlie: Do all the people in our audience know that?

Puppeteer: I don't know—but I hope so. That's why we are here—to help everyone learn about God's love. Let me read one verse that explains it very well. (*Reads John 3:16*.)
I have it written on this chart. Let's put it up here so everyone can read it. That should give our valentine decorations some real meaning. (*Put chart on stand or tape to outside of stage*.)

Charlie: I'm going to look for that girl. She would like to learn about real love too.
(*Charlie exits and the narrator summarizes God's love and invites people to accept Christ by faith*.)

THE KING AND THE GIFT

A three-act puppet play based on a tale from medieval times.

Characters:
- Narrator
- Herald
- King
- Peasant Boy (Philip)
- Several peasant children

Props:
- trumpet
- baskets
- little plastic fruits and vegetables
- seeds of various kinds
- throne

Scene One: Village street in medieval times

Narrator stands at side of stage aperture

Narrator: Once upon a time there was a king who had a beautiful palace and a lovely garden. One day—(*Interrupted by trumpet.*)

One day the king announced that there was going to be a harvest feast. It was announced throughout his kingdom something like this: (*Narrator steps aside as the Herald enters stage from right.*)

Herald: (*Holds up the scroll of news.*)
Hear Ye! Hear ye! His Royal Majesty, the king, invites everyone to a grand feast. It shall be held on the first day of the autumn, on September the twenty-first at the palace gardens. Come one! Come all to his majesty's party.
(*Herald leaves stage crying "Hear ye! Hear ye!" as voice fades away.*)
(*Two boys enter from left.*)

Peasant Boy 1: Did you hear that?

Peasant Boy 2: (*Imitating horn.*) Toot-too-de-too-too.

PB 1: Not that, dummy, the message.

PB 2: Oh, that! Yeah . . .

PB 1: Are ya going?

PB 2: To what?

PB 1: To the party?

PB 2: What party?

PB 1: The one the king is having!

PB 2: The king is having a party?

PB 1: I thought you were listening!

PB 2: Yeah—but I musta missed something.

PB 1:	I think you missed it all!
PB 2:	What did I miss?
PB 1:	Oh, just that his majesty is having a special party and we are invited.
PB 2:	We?
PB 1:	We! I'm going. Wanna come along?
PB 2:	(*Uncertainly.*) Yeah . . . sure. (*Philip enters the stage from right. He is carrying a basket of rolls, covered with a checkered cloth.*)
PB 1:	Hi, Philip! Did ya hear what the king's herald said?
Philip:	Yes, I sure did. Sounds neat!
PB 1:	Are ya going?
Philip:	Well, I haven't thought about it yet! I wonder what Mother would think about my going?
PB 2:	Mother?! You ask your mother about everything?
Philip:	I sure do. Don't you?
PB 2:	Aw . . . (*Voice dies off.*).
PB 1:	What's in your basket, Philip?
Philip:	Some of the rolls Mother made. I'm taking them to market.
PB 2:	Ya got one for me? (*He tries to help himself.*)
PB 1:	Get away from that basket.
PB 2:	But I'm hungry.
PB 1:	Then buy one!
Philip:	Would you care to buy one? They are only three pence each.
PB 2:	Naw. (*Retreats, acts disinterested.*)
Philip:	Well, I'll see you fellas around. I must hurry on to market. Since there is only Mother and me, I must help her all I can. (*He pats top of basket to make sure rolls are okay, then leaves stage.*)
PB 1:	I don't think Philip will make it to the party. He's got too much to do.

(Curtain)

Scene Two: Vine-covered wall of king's garden.

Narrator stands at side of stage aperture

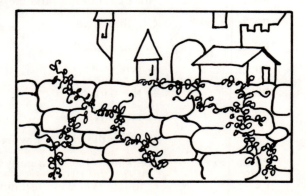

Narrator: Finally the big day arrived. People came from all over the land to the king's harvest feast. The castle grounds and gardens were crowded with peasants. Then, during the festivities, his royal majesty announced . . . (*Interrupted by trumpet.*)

. . . His royal majesty announced a contest.
(*Narrator steps aside as the Herald enters stage from right.*)

Herald: (*Calls out to crowd.*) Hear ye! Hear ye! His royal majesty, the king, invites all of the children to go through the palace gardens and find whatever they consider the very best gift there. Then, at mid-afternoon, all choices shall be presented to his royal majesty, the king. The reward for the best gift will be presented at sunset before the royal throne.
(*Herald leaves stage on right.*)
(*A rustle of leaves and twigs snapping, is heard in the background as the children go through the garden. Children emerge from left of stage, one at a time, and move across stage to exit right. Each one is carrying a different kind of produce, such as a pumpkin, a bunch of grapes, a carrot, a tomato, a bouquet of flowers, or a nut. Some of these products could be carried in baskets. Last of all, Philip comes along with his basket and the checkered cloth over it. The basket contains seeds. He humbly crosses stage and exits also.*)
(*Curtain*)

Scene Three: Throne room

Herald enters from right.

Herald: (*Announces.*) Hear ye! Hear ye! The court announces the arrival of his majesty, the king. Long live the king!

Crowd: (*Off-stage—responds.*) Long live the king!
(*King appears from right and seats himself on his throne. Herald moves to center stage to be announcer.*)

King: Welcome, my people.
(*Peasant children move shyly onto stage from left.*)

King: It has been a long day. Many fine gifts were brought to me from the palace garden. I am pleased with them all. You are entitled to see who the winner is. You! (*Pointing at Philip.*)—the lad with the covered basket—step forward.
(*Philip trembles but steps forward. Bows before king.*)

King: Lad, what do you have in your basket?

Philip: I . . . I . . . Your Majesty, I . . .

King:	Show the people what you have.
Philip:	(*Removes cloth and takes out a seed*.) Your Majesty, I searched and searched all afternoon through your beautiful garden and . . . and everything was so beautiful! Oh, how wonderful it must be to live here and walk through that garden every day! Your Majesty—if you wish to have another garden as beautiful as this—you will have to have seeds to plant next year. So I brought some seeds from the plants in your garden. (*Offers the basket to the king who takes it*.) I am ashamed, Sire, for the seeds are brown, and hard and ugly—not pretty like the other gifts. I hope you will forgive me, Your majesty, but this is my gift to you.
King:	Forgiven? My son, I have considered well, if you had not brought the seeds, I could not have a garden like that again next year. You have chosen the very finest gift of all—for yours is a gift of thought and love. You are the one who shall receive the highest reward . . . I would like you to come live at the palace—and bring your family, too—for I would like you to be my gardener. (*Philip bows low. Others bow. King stands.*) (*Curtain*)
Narrator:	Trying to find something to please the king was a very difficult task— but the king was a wise man and understood why Philip chose the seeds. We have someone far more important to us than a king. God is our maker, our ruler—and like a mighty king over us, He wants us to honor Him. But there is no way we can please Him unless we belong to Him. Then He wants us to bring our gifts to Him. The world is His garden and we are to bring the seeds to Him. The seeds are other people who need to be saved, so that they also may go out and bring forth other seeds to Him. Will you bring others to Jesus?

King with child.

THE SEARCH FOR A TALENT

A one-act puppet play on self-evaluation.

Characters:
Wally
Mert
Mr. Jones
Teacher

Props:
drum
drumsticks
toy piano
three small balls
pebbles
container with water
paper heart

As scene opens two boys enter stage from opposite sides.

Mert: Hi, Wally.

Wally: Oh, hi, Mert. Say have you heard about the talent show that's coming up next month?

Mert: Talent show? What talent show?

Wally: You know. Remember the one our neighborhood was planning to have at the grade school this summer? (*Use appropriate season.*)

Mert: Oh, yeah, now I remember. I guess I'd really forgotten about that. Just what is it, Wally?

Wally: Oh, you know. Everybody, er—I mean a lot of folks put on a show. They take turns showing off their talents. Some . . .

Mert: (*Interrupts.*) Like what?

Wally: Mert! Don't interrupt me.

Mert: Sorry, Wally.

Wally: I was going to tell you . . .

Mert: (*Interrupts.*) Tell me what?

Wally: Oh, boy! There you go again. Are you ready to listen? (*Folds hands and waits.*)

Mert: Yes.

Wally: Good. Now, what was I saying?

Mert: You were going to tell me . . . (*Pause, scratches head.*) . . . you were going to tell me . . .

Wally: Oh, yes, I was going to tell you about some of the different talents.

Mert: Okay.

Wally: Well, people sing, or read poetry, or play, or dance, or show off their skills.

Mert: Like what?

Wally: Like stamp collections or making furniture, or canning dill pickles.

Mert: Canning dill pickles? Yuk! (*He shakes head.*)

Wally: Mert! (*Mert laughs.*) What's so funny about that?

Mert: (*Clutches throat.*) Sour pickles as a talent. Yuk!

Wally: Don't laugh, Mert. Who knows what talent you may have? Bye. (*Walks off-stage.*)

Mert: Now, how do you like that? He can't even take a joke. He thinks I don't have a talent. Ha. I'll show him. I think I'll enter that show and show him! Yes sir. I'll show him. (*Pauses thoughtfully.*) Now, let's see, what will I do? (*Pause.*) What can I do? (*Pause.*) I'll do something I know. I'll sing. Everybody can sing! Er . . . some people can sing. All I need is to practice. Okay, here goes. (*Sings badly. Makes several attempts.*) That will never do! Maybe singing is not my talent. I know, I'll play an instrument. Let's see. What's easy? Oh, yes, the drums. No notes there. All I have to do is use rhythm and I've got tons of that. (*Runs off-stage and reenters with drum. Begins to play very badly. Changes position. Tries again. Throws sticks down and plops head on drum.*) I'll never make it as a drummer. Oh, boy!
(*Looks down. Picks up drumstick.*) Say!! Maybe I could twirl a baton— like this. (*Tries it—falls to the ground.*) It's no use.
Well, I can't give up now. I've got almost a month to find my talent. I know. I'll play the piano. Where is that granddaddy piano with the colored keys? (*Runs off-stage—rolls in toy piano with colored keys. Plays terribly.*) Yuk! It sounds bad to me and I'm not a musician. Say, that's my problem. I'm not a musician. Okay, I'll try something else. Hmmm . . . (*Pauses to think.*) I know. Where are those three balls? I'll try juggling. That should be easy. (*Runs off, comes back with three balls and tries to juggle. Doesn't do it well.*) I give up. Maybe it would be easier to do a collection. Let's see! What are there lots of? Lots of? Ah . . . mice. Nope. Ah . . . bugs. That's it, bugs! Never a scarcity of those. Watch out, bugs! Here I come! Raid! (*Runs off-stage.*)

Wally: (*Entering from opposite side.*) Raid? Did I hear someone cry, "Raid"? (*Scratches his head.*) Wonder where Mert went. He sure has lots of energy. (*Exits.*)

Mert: (*Entering from opposite side.*) Yikes, look at all of these bugs in this jar. Now, all I have to do is mount them—after I kill them and identify them. (*Looks in jar.*) Poor bugs! Yuk. I don't like this idea too much. (*Dumps bugs out.*)
I've gotta do something. Maybe I can collect something that isn't alive. Yeah! Rocks. They won't bite nor have to be killed. I'll just kick up a few rocks and identify them. (*Goes off with head down scuffling along. Returns with armload of pebbles. Puts them down.*)
Let's see! Now, to identify them. This one is . . . no, this one is a sandstone, and this one is a mudstone, and this one is a . . . a . . . it's all wet, it must be a whetstone. And here's marble, and here's a pumice stone. Is it really? If it is, it will float. I'll try it. (*Runs off. Returns with glass jar of water. Drops rock in. It sinks.*) Oh, brother. Maybe it's this one. (*Drops another in. It sinks.*) Nope. This one? (*Drops it, it sinks too.*)

Wally: (*Enters.*) Hi, Mert. What are you doing? (*Looks in jar.*) Washing rocks?

Mert:	(*Disgusted.*) Yeah, it's my talent.
Wally:	Oh, Mert. (*Laughs his way off-stage.*)
Mert:	(*Puts head in hands.*) Oh, brother. I don't have any talent. I wish I could do just one thing well. (*Keeps head down.*)
Mr. Jones:	(*Enters.*) Mert? Is that you? I thought I'd find you here. Say, you know we are having a talent show next month and I'm chairman for the program. I've been asking around to find the best master of cere-monies and people I've talked to have suggested your name. They say you have the talent for a tough job like that. I think so, too. How about it, Mert? Would you be willing to use your talent as a master of ceremonies for us? We really want it to be a good program and with your help it will be.
Mert:	My talent is . . . is speaking? I never thought about that. Sure! Sure! I'll be glad to help in the talent show. Thanks for asking me, Mr. Jones.
Mr. Jones:	God gives each of us a talent, Mert. We just have to be willing to find and use the one He has given us, and not wish for something that belongs to another.

(Curtain)

(*Teacher or one of puppeteers comes up to the side of the stage and calls to puppets.*)

Teacher:	Say, don't go away! What do you mean, God has given each of us a talent? I really want to know more about this and I'm sure the children here want to know more, too. Please come out. (*Waits.*) Please. (*Cautiously all three appear.*) Oh, thank you. Now . . . (*All three take a bow.*) No! (*All three disappear quickly; straight down.*) Oh, c'mon now. I want to talk to you. (*All three cautiously appear again.*) There! I'm glad you came back. Aren't you glad they did, boys and girls? (*Pause for audience reaction—trust it's favorable.*) I have some questions to ask you. (*Mert and Wally look at Mr. Jones in the center, expecting him to be the one to answer.*) My first question is this, How do you know God gives each of us some talent?
Mr. Jones:	It's in the Bible.
Wally:	Where, Mr. Jones?
Mert:	Don't interrupt, Wally. Go ahead, Mr. Jones. (*Mert is glad to correct Wally.*)
Mr. Jones:	Thank you, Mert. (*Nods toward him.*) I'm glad you asked that, Wally. First Corinthians 12 speaks of some of these gifts. God's Holy Spirit gives to each Christian just what God wants that person to have. Every Christian is a member of the spiritual body of Christ. Some have talents for teaching, or healing, or governing—that's being able to manage large groups of people.
Teacher:	What talents do you think these boys and girls might have?
Mr. Jones:	I don't know, but there's one special talent God wants everyone to have.
Wally & Mert:	Really? What's that?
Teacher:	Yes, what is that? I'd like to try for the best thing God has for me—and I'm sure these boys and girls would, too. What is it?

Mr. Jones:	(*Goes down and comes up holding a red heart.*) It's love. L-O-V-E, love! The next chapter, First Corinthians 13, tells us about love. (*Read or recite I Cor. 13:4–7.*) God's Word says we should all learn to love better.
Teacher:	That's a real challenge. All the boys and girls can work on that.
Mr. Jones:	They sure can.
Mert:	(*Looking at kids.*) Do you suppose some of them have enough love already?
Wally:	Oh, Mert, of course. (*Facetiously.*) Just like you! Do you think they are satisfied already?
Mr. Jones:	(*Laughing.*) I think, if they're honest, they would all admit that they are still working at it. Aren't you, kids? (*To them.*) Keep working. (*All three disappear.*)
Teacher:	(*To children.*) Do you feel like Mert? You really don't know what talents or gifts are yours? God will show us our gifts. Let's not forget that God wants us all to learn to love others as He loves us. We want to be our very best for God.

A Christmas Reminder

A one-act puppet play.

Characters:
- Chris
- Dad
- Mom

Props:
- small Christmas tree
- box with lid
- little lamb
- ornaments (see script for various kinds)

Scene One: Living room

Stage is empty. Christmas music begins to play. "O Tannenbaum"

Dad comes in wearing cap, carrying a Christmas tree and sets it up on stage left. Looks at it approvingly. Leaves.

Mom comes in with a white box tied with red ribbon (in the design of a cross).She places the box under the tree. Stands back to see if it looks just right. Leaves.

Chris: (*Enters from stage right, wearing cap.*) Oh, goody! Christmas is coming! I can hardly wait! Dad must have put the tree up just a while ago. (*Goes up to examine it.*) Smells great! (*Dances around. Notices box under tree. Stops.*) What's this? A present already? (*Picks it up and shakes it. Examines it carefully.*) I wonder what it is and who put it here? I wonder how long we have to wait to open it? I think I'll go ask Dad. (*Exits to stage right.*)

(*Dad enters from stage left, cap removed, with some silver stars to put on tree. Chris enters, capless, from right after Dad has hung all the stars.*)

Chris: Oh, there you are, Dad, I've been looking for you.

Dad: Hi, Chris. What was it you wanted?

Chris: I don't remember. May I help you decorate?

Dad: Certainly.

Mom: (*Enters from stage left, carrying some felt birds.*) Hello, Chris. I'm glad you came home in time to help us decorate the tree.

Dad: This year, your Mother and I have decided to use only symbolic decorations. We think that you are old enough to appreciate their significance. Do you see these silver stars?

Chris: Yes.

Dad: In Italy, some people trim their trees only with silver stars. Why do you suppose they do that?

Chris:	I don't know.
Dad:	Think a minute. Think back to the first Christmas.
Chris:	Ohhh . . . you mean when Jesus was born? There was a star then.
Dad:	That's right, this is to remind us of the special star God put in the sky to guide the wise men to the baby Jesus. (*Pause*.) I forgot something important. I'll go get it. (*Exit*.)
Chris:	What do you have, Mom?
Mom:	Do you see these little birds? (*She and Chris put birds on the tree*.) In some countries where winters are very long and cold—such as in Sweden—people are concerned about caring for God's creatures. They put out food for the birds in the winter. So they put birds on their tree to remind them of God's beautiful little creatures.
Chris:	Could we feed some birds this winter?
Mom:	I don't see why not.
Dad:	(*Returns with crèche*.) Chris, this goes along with the stars. You've seen these before, haven't you?
Chris:	(*Looking at it*.) I know what that is—a manger scene—with wise men, too. Are you going to put that on the bookshelf?
Dad:	No, Chris, under the tree. Each day you may move the wise men a little closer to the baby Jesus. That should help remind you that the real purpose of Christmas is to worship God.
Chris:	(*Curious*.) Why did you put it beside that big present? What's in there? Who's it for?
Dad:	Wait a minute! You ask too many questions. We'll get to that later. Now, will we be able to see this if I leave it here? (*All survey the arrangement*.)
Chris:	Sure.
Mom:	Yes, that's good. (*Leaves room, talking on way out*.) Now, I believe there's another important decoration for our tree this year. . . . (*Returns with snowflakes*.) These should remind us of verses in God's Word.
Chris:	Snowflakes?
Dad:	Yes, son, can you think of any verses? (*They all put snowflakes on tree*.)
Chris:	Uh . . . ummm . . . Uh . . . No, give me a clue.
Dad:	One verse was to Noah after the flood.
Mom:	In one verse David talks about the weather.
Dad:	In another verse Job spoke about treasures and snow.
Chris:	Oh, c'mon, I don't know any of those. You all know your Bibles better than I do.
Dad:	Okay, to Noah: "As long as the earth remains, there will be springtime and harvest, cold and heat, winter and summer, day and night."
Mom:	David said, "He [God] gives snow like wool; . . .
Dad:	Job said, "Have you entered the treasuries of the snow?"

Chris:	But what does snow have to do with Jesus' birth?
Mom:	Why did Jesus come?
Chris:	Because He loved us enough to come and die for our sins.
Dad:	Right, Chris. The Bible says God can make sins whiter than snow. That means He takes them away.
Mom:	How do you like our tree now? (*They all survey the tree.*)
Chris:	It looks great! And everything means something.
Dad:	Yes. Now Chris, would you like to know what is in the box underneath the tree?
Chris:	Boy! Would I! Do we get to open it now? Do we?
Dad:	Yes, it's a reminder for all of us. (*Chris gets box.*)
Mom:	Notice the colors and design.
Chris:	White and red. Those are Christmas colors.
Mom:	Can you think of something else that these colors might stand for?
Chris:	Hmmm. White for the snow—our sins taken away. Red for . . . uh . . . red for Jesus's blood that fell when He died for us. (*Looks at ribbon on box.*) And this ribbon looks like a cross.
Dad:	Good, son. Now what do you suppose is inside?
Chris:	(*Eagerly.*) Okay! (*Takes top off.*) A little lamb! (*Takes it out.*) Who's it for?
Mom & Dad:	All of us.
Dad:	It's our reminder of a Bible verse: "Behold, the Lamb of God who takes away the sin of the world."
Mom:	That's what Christmas is all about. It's to celebrate Jesus' birthday, because He came to be the Savior of the world.
Chris:	Why don't we keep it under the tree this Christmas so we won't forget?
Mom & Dad:	Good idea.
Mom & Dad:	Merry Christmas, son.
Chris:	Merry Christmas. This will be the best Christmas yet! (*Play music for "Joy to the World."*) (*Curtain*)

PATTERNS FOR ORNAMENTS

Birds:
Use felt to make birds: red is a good color to use (for cardinals), or brown birds (song sparrows) could also work.

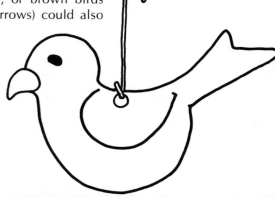

Little Lamb:
Make cardboard body. Color legs black with felt pen. Glue on cotton balls. Add black felt ears and black felt eyes.

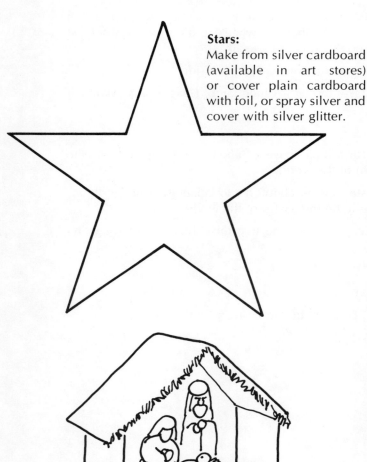

Stars:
Make from silver cardboard (available in art stores) or cover plain cardboard with foil, or spray silver and cover with silver glitter.

The little Christmas tree with reminders of the real meaning of Christmas.

Crèche: Use a very small set (available in Bible bookstores or variety shops), or make a small set. It should be in one piece for ease in handling by the puppet.

Two and One-Half Big Surprises

A one-act puppet play on the importance of being responsible.

Characters:
Mother
Tommy
Susie

Props:
two boxes with lids and bows
(one orange and one green bow)
dictionary
plastic daffodil
flowerpot
watering pot
football gear, baseball hat, ball, and bat
sign: MUCH, MUCH LATER
sign: LATER, MUCH LATER
sign: SPRING

Scene One: Home interior or a plain backdrop

Mother enters stage with two big packages.

Mother:	Children! Tommy! Susie! Come see what I have for you. (*Children come running.*)
Tommy:	What is it, Mother?
Susie:	Is it a surprise?
Tommy:	A present?
Susie:	Oh, Mother! For us? Thank you. (*Mother nods yes.*) May we open the boxes?
Mother:	Of course you may, if you promise to do one thing for me.
Children:	Yes, Mother. What is it?
Mother:	You know that Father and I have been trying to help you children learn about responsibility.
Children:	(*Anxiously.*) Yes, Mother.
Mother:	Now, don't get too anxious. I'm not finished yet. But I will tell you this—the box contains something that can grow.
Susie:	Oh, Mother, a pet?
Tommy:	A puppy?
Mother:	No, children, not in a box like this. Maybe pets could come later. But, this will help you learn about responsibility. Will you promise that you will try your best to faithfully take care of what is in the boxes?
Children:	Yes, Mother, we will! We will! May we open our boxes now?

77

Mother:	Promise?
Children:	Promise!
Mother:	All right, you may open the boxes now. Susie, this one is yours, with the green bow, and Tommy, this one with the orange bow is yours. (*Both children pull off bows and lift lids off boxes.*) (*Children peering into box—look up surprised.*)
Susie:	Mother! There's nothing in it.
Tommy:	But dirt.
Mother:	Oh, yes, there is—look carefully. (*Both children look again.*)
Susie:	Oh, I think I see something.
Tommy:	I see something round like a mushroom . . . or a golf ball.
Mother:	I think you've found it.
Susie:	What is it?
Tommy:	I thought you said it was alive.
Mother:	I said it was something that could grow—in a way it is sleeping right now.
Susie:	Sleeping?
Tommy:	Sleeping!! (*Really peeks in.*)
Mother:	Yes, sort of. Look at the inside of the box lid and see if you can find some directions. (*Both children look at their box lids.*)
Susie:	Here's something written on mine.
Tommy:	Mine has directions, too.
Mother:	Now, you both are good readers. If I leave now—would you each be able to take care of your surprise?
Children:	Oh, yes, Mother! Thank you for . . . whatever.
Mother:	(*Chuckling.*) We shall see who knows what it is. Have fun children. Remember, you promised to take good care of your present. (*Exits.*)
Tommy:	Oh, boy!! (*Begins to read.*) The little bulb that you have in the box is a . . . an . . . uh . . .
Susie:	The little bulb that you have in the box is a . . . a . . . daffodil. (*Mispronounced day-fō-dill.*)
Tommy:	A what? I never heard of that!
Susie:	Neither have I.
Tommy:	Maybe it's from Russia or somewhere far away, maybe from Uganda—I just heard about that.
Susie:	Oh, Tommy, maybe we're saying it wrong.
Tommy:	We could look it up in the dictionary.
Susie:	Yeah! We could. I never thought of that. It might even tell us what it's like.
Tommy:	And especially how to pronounce it. I'll go get the dictionary. (*Exits.*)

78

Susie:	(*Reads again.*) The little bulb that you have in the box is a . . . a . . . da-fod'ill, da-fod-ill. Oh, brother! (*Tommy reenters with dictionary.*)
Susie:	Did you find it?
Tommy:	Not yet! I just got here.
Susie:	Let's do it together. (*Both start looking.*) D, D, D-a. (*She is locating aloud.*)
Tommy:	D-a-f (*Locates aloud also.*). Daffy!
Susie:	Silly!
Tommy:	(*Surprised.*) That's exactly what it means! How did you know?
Susie:	(*Looks at dictionary.*) Oh, brother! Here it is! (*Pronounces slowly and carefully.*) Daf'ə–dil It's a flower.
Tommy:	What does the dictionary say? (*He leans over and reads aloud.*) A plant with a yellow flower and long narrow leaves.
Susie:	I've seen those before. They bloom in the spring.
Tommy:	But we don't have a spring.
Susie:	The time before summer, silly, not a well.
Tommy:	Oh, let's read our directions.
Susie:	Okay. (*Both read quietly.*)
Tommy:	(*Looks up and away.*) There's no hurry—it's a long time till spring.
Susie:	But, Tommy, we need to plant them now. It says to plant them in the fall, *before* winter comes.
Tommy:	I will. (*He gets up to leave.*)
Susie:	Where are you going?
Tommy:	I promised the guys I'd play football this afternoon. I gotta go. (*Starts off the stage.*)
Susie:	When are you going to plant your daffodil?
Tommy:	(*From off-stage.*) Later.
Susie:	(*Reads directions aloud to herself.*) Place bulb in dirt or cover with pebbles . . . I'll plant mine right now. (*She picks up box and goes off-stage. Returns with bulb in flowerpot. Sets it down.*) There. Little bulb, grow and grow. I can hardly wait. (*Exits.*)
Tommy:	(*Enters wearing football outfit.*) Oh, my bulb. I should plant it, but I guess tomorrow will be soon enough. (*Exits.*)
Interlude:	Hold up the sign that says:

LATER, MUCH LATER

Susie:	(*Enters.*) Hi, little plant, I see you are beginning to grow. (*Then she looks at Tommy's box.*) Oh, poor little bulb. Tommy hasn't planted you yet. (*Exits.*)
Tommy:	(*Enters, crossing stage in a hurry.*) Boy, I hope the guys haven't already left for the ice skating rink. I sure like winter. We can go ice skating and play hockey! (*Looks at box*) I should plant that bulb soon. (*Exits.*)
Mother:	(*Enters, looks at box and flowerpot.*) Well, I can see who is doing the best job of keeping their promise and learning responsibility. I won't say anything to Tommy. I think the bulb will teach him all he will need to know. (*Looks into Susie's flowerpot. Exits.*)
Interlude:	Holds up sign that says:

Push some green leaves up through the flowerpot so it looks as though it has grown.

Tommy:	(*Enters with baseball hat, ball and bat.*) Boy! I love spring and baseball. (*Glances at box.*) Oops—I should plant that! (*Exits.*)
Susie:	(*Enters and waters her plant.*) Hi, there daffodil mine. You're really doing fine! How's that!! I made a poem! (*Repeats it. Exits.*)
Interlude:	Hold up sign that says:

Put a daffodil in the flowerpot. It might work to push one up out of center of pot from hole in the bottom.

Mother:	(*Enters and calls.*) Children! Tommy! Susie! Come here, please. (*Children enter.*)
Tommy:	Hi, Mom!
Susie:	Hi, Mother. What is it?
Mother:	Do you remember our surprise last fall?
Children:	Yes, Mother.
Mother:	What did you get?
Tommy:	A bulb.
Susie:	A flower.

Mother:	You're both right, but what makes the difference between a bulb and a flower?
Susie:	Caring for it, planting it, watering it, and talking to it.
Mother:	Well, planting and watering, yes, but I'm not too sure about the talking bit (*Chuckles.*). And what was the promise you made?
Susie:	To care for it.
Tommy:	I don't remember, but I think you said plant it.
Mother:	I asked you both to promise to faithfully take care of what was in the boxes. Remember now?
Children:	Yes.
Mother:	And you had to read the instructions and care for it.
Children:	Yes, Mother.
Mother:	Did you do that?
Susie:	I did. (*Tommy hangs head.*)
Mother:	Susie has a beautiful daffodil. You will be able to keep this year after year if you continue caring for it as you have been. Tommy, look in your box. (*He does.*) What do you have?
Tommy:	It's still a bulb, Mother.
Mother:	Is it? Touch it, Tommy.
Tommy:	(*Touches it.*) Yuck! It's all mushy.
Mother:	Yes, you waited too long, Tommy. You didn't bother to keep your promise. Now, I have something else for you, children.
Susie:	Another present, Mother?
Tommy:	Another surprise?
Mother:	Yes, another surprise.
Children:	Do we both get it?
Mother:	(*Thoughtfully.*) Well, what do you think I should do? (*Curtain*)
Application:	(*Teacher talks to the children in the audience.*) We all have many responsibilities to learn, don't we? (Yes) Do you think both children learned? (Yes) What did Susie learn? (She obeyed and a daffodil grew.) What did Tommy learn? (He kept putting it off and a daffodil did not grow.) What did Mother learn about them? (Susie kept her promise; Tommy did not.) Do you think she has another surprise for them? (Yes) Will both of them get it? (We don't know what Mother will decide.) What do you think it could be? (Children will name things they would like to have—maybe a dog.) God gives us opportunities and responsibilities too. Often it is something that our mothers and fathers want us to do. Don't put it off. Do it soon and do it well. You will be much happier if you obey right away.

The Empty House

A puppet play for Halloween-time or anytime.

To illustrate that we need Jesus to control our life so that problems won't overwhelm us.

To be read by a narrator while the puppets pantomine the parts.

Characters:
Little House
several neighbor houses
Pride
Envy and Jealousy (Twins)
Love of Money
Bad Language
Narrator

Scene One: Pleasant neighborhood

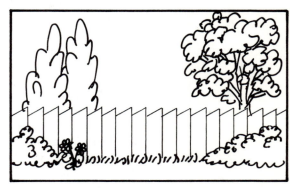

Once upon a time there was a very happy Little House . It lived on a street called Straight and it had many kind neighborhood houses. Each was different to look at, but all were happy. (*Play joyful music. Show several other homes by putting them up one at a time beside the Little House, then taking them down again. Alternate from side to side if you like.*)

It was pleasant and sunny on the street called Straight. Each little house had much for which to be thankful: flowers, fresh air, sunshine, good neighbors, clean talk, peace, good music and laughter. Everything good surrounded them. And the little houses thought good thoughts day after day. (*Play soft soothing music.*)

But one day, the Little House heard a loud, loud noise. (*Sound effects of loud noise.*) It turned to look behind itself to another street. (*Turn house partway around.*) Across the back fence was another row of houses on an avenue called Crooked. The grass was much greener on the other side of the fence and all of the houses there seemed much bigger and more important than the houses on Straight Street.

"Oh," thought the Little House, "Wouldn't it be nice to go over there where the grass is so much greener, and everything looks more important. It sounds like such fun over there, but it is quite a bit shadier there than on our street—so I can't really tell. If only I could get a better look. Maybe I can turn around (*Grunts.*) and look that way. (*The Little House turns.*) Wouldn't it be nice to visit over there? Maybe I could. (*Tries to move, but can't.*) Ugh! This is hard work! I can't seem to get free to go. This is tiring me out. Oh, (*Big sigh.*). Maybe I could rest just a bit." (*Yawns.*) (*Put shades down. Tilt chimmey. Straighten mouth.*)
(*Play a lullaby.*)

(*Curtain*)

83

Scene Two: Home interior.

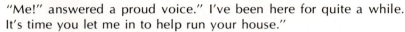

The Little House was very tired and very close to sleep when it heard a noise at the door . . .
(*Knock.*)

"Who's there?" called the Little House.

"Me!" answered a proud voice." I've been here for quite a while. It's time you let me in to help run your house."

"Oh," the Little House replied."Come in. I didn't realize you were out there waiting. (*Pride comes in, strutting around.*) Have you really been waiting there very long?"

"Oh, yes," answered Pride with a happy bounce. (*Pride bounces.*) "I've been trying for ever so long just to get my foot in the door, so to speak, but you were so busy enjoying the good things on Straight Street that I couldn't get your attention until you took a look at Crooked Avenue.

"Oh," the Little House answered, "I wasn't aware of that. I've been feeling rather empty and sorry for myself lately. Maybe it's good that you came."

"Of course, it's good that I came," Pride replied happily."You need me. I'll be able to help you brag and feel good. That's my job, you know. You will soon feel as good as all your neighbors and maybe even better. Then . . ."

But just then he was interrupted by a knock on the door (*Knock.*) and, even though the Little House was not expecting any more company—in fact having Pride there seemed to be enough to fill the house—Pride did not seem surprised.

"Who's there?" called the Little House.

"Just us. We've been waiting to come in after Pride. We are good friends of his and usually go where he goes. May we come in?"

"Yes, come in." said the Little House as two strange-looking creatures strutted in. (*Envy and Jealousy enter together.*) "But who are you? And why are you here?" (*Envy & Jealousy strut around, peeking out of his windows and watching at the door.*) The creatures acted so suspiciously that the Little House began to worry. But he thought to himself, he really shouldn't worry, because, after all, he had been wondering what life was all about on the other side. Now he could learn about the reasons for the loud, loud noises on Crooked Avenue. These characters were apparently from the other side of the fence where the grass seemed greener.

"Don't you recognize us? We belong together. We are Envy and Jealousy—you can tell that by our green eyes. We use them constantly to help you know what's going on in your neighborhood. Then we let Pride know so he can tell you what to do about it. We don't want anybody, anybody—you get that—to have things that you don't have. You should be able to keep up to the Joneses, so to speak, with our diligent help. You really need us, you know, or Pride might try to make you feel sad. We can help you feel like working hard at everything. You will always want more. Then . . ."

Envy and Jealousy were interrupted by a knock on the door (*Knock.*)

84

and even though the Little House was certainly not expecting any more company—Pride, Envy and Jealousy were not surprised to hear another knock at the door.

"Who's there?" called the Little House.

"It's me!" came the answer. "You'll love me!" (*Love of Money enters, jingling.*)

"How did you find me?" "Why did you want to come here? You are beautiful!"

"Oh, yes, I know," answered the creature. "I am beautiful. I wear a good disguise to show off my outside beauty. I usually follow Envy and Jealousy around, and, as you know, they follow Pride. We work best together. In fact, we wouldn't survive if we were alone. Dreadful thought really."

"I suppose so." (*The four creatures bump into one another, struggle, grunting noises of dissatisfaction.*) (*Noises get a bit louder.*)

"I didn't know that it would be like this on Crooked Avenue," (*sigh*) "It was noisy—but I thought the noise was a good sound. Now I'm not so sure. (*Noise continues to grow.*) In fact, I don't like it! Not at all!" (*Knock is heard above din.*)

"Who's there?" (*Pause.*) "Who's there?" (*Pause.*)

"Me, you dummy." (*Or use other expression that shows lack of respect but is not offensive to your audience.*) "Let me in! If you don't, I'll bust in anyway," (*Bad Language enters.*) "These other stupid creatures are my buddies and we stick together—even though they are accepted before I am. (*Bragging.*) I'm just as good as they are. You need me, small fry. I help drive others away so you can have some peace." (*The creatures' struggle grow still louder.*)

"Oh," groaned the Little House. "Why did I ever look over at Crooked Avenue anyway? These aren't good characters. These aren't good sounds. I don't like this company. The grass is *not* greener on this side of the fence. I liked the sunshine on Straight Street. I liked my neighbors there. I liked the good thoughts, and clean talk and peace and quiet. I like the nice music and the joyful laughter. (*Pause.*) I need help! My house needs cleaning! Who will help me clean it up? (*Pause.*) I know, my builder. I'll ask him. Now, out! Out! All of you out." "OUT! OUT! OUT!" (*As he speaks this command over and over, close the curtain quickly, and reopen it again showing the Little House, shades drawn, back on Straight Street surrounded by the other happy homes. He rocks as though tossing and turning in his sleep with a bad dream.*)

"Little House! Little House!" the other little houses exclaimed. "Wake up!" (*Shades open.*) "Were you dreaming?"

"Oh," said the Little House. "Oh, I hope so. I hope so! It was dreadful. I don't want ever to be anywhere else but right here on Straight Street where the sun is always shining and I have good neighbors. Thank you for waking me up."

(*Curtain*)

HOUSE PATTERN

You will need the following materials:
   cardboard
   brads
   construction paper
   crayons, markers, or tempera paint
   popsicle sticks

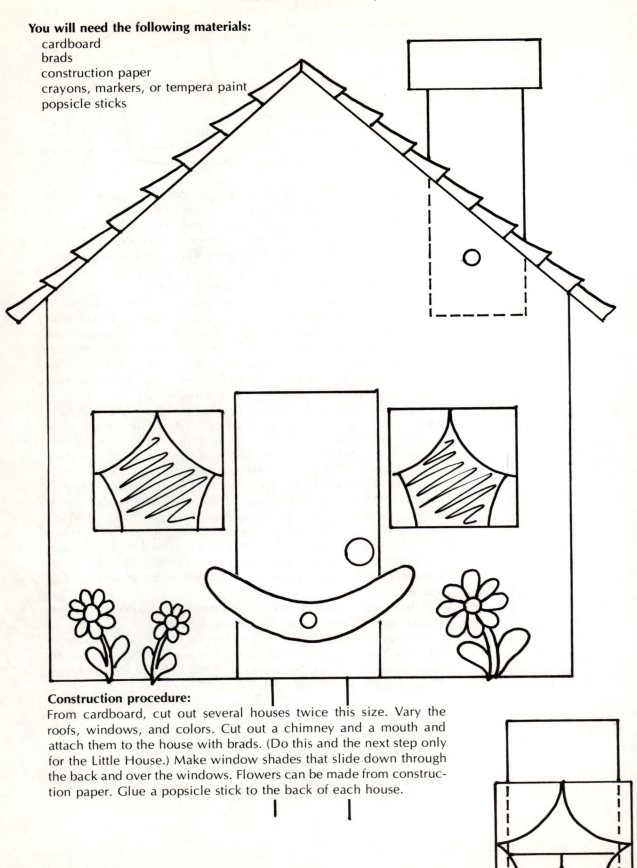

Construction procedure:
From cardboard, cut out several houses twice this size. Vary the roofs, windows, and colors. Cut out a chimney and a mouth and attach them to the house with brads. (Do this and the next step only for the Little House.) Make window shades that slide down through the back and over the windows. Flowers can be made from construction paper. Glue a popsicle stick to the back of each house.

DIRECTIONS FOR MAKING PUPPETS FOR "THE EMPTY HOUSE"

You will need the following materials:
styrofoam balls
dowels
fake fur
felt
movable eyes
gold sequins
aluminum foil
cotton balls
fringe balls
cardboard (lightweight)
fabric glue
straight pins
gray spray paint

Construction procedure:
Insert dowel into bottom of styrofoam ball. Use appropriate materials for individual puppets.

Pride: Cover styrofoam ball with white fake fur. Glue on with fabric glue. Make a hat by covering cardboard with black felt. Glue on movable eyes, a felt mouth, and a fringe ball nose.

Envy and Jealousy: Cover ball with green fake fur. Glue on green eyes (of a differing shade of green). Glue on fringe ball nose.

Love of Money: Cover ball with aluminum foil. Attach gold sequins for eyes and hair with straight pins. Glue on fringe ball nose. (This can be done by cutting a circle out of the foil where the nose is to be placed.)

Bad Language: Glue cotton balls to ball. Spray paint gray. Let dry. Glue on felt exclamation points, etc.

PRIDE

ENVY AND JEALOUSY

LOVE OF MONEY

BAD LANGUAGE

Church of St. Vincent de Paul
900 Madison Ave.
Albany, N. Y.